D0006659

ODDBALL

Other books by Sarah Andersen

Adulthood Is a Myth

Big Mushy Happy Lump

Herding Cats

Fangs

ODDBALL

A "Sarah's Scribbles" collection

Sarah Andersen

Andrews McMeel
PUBLISHING®

AGING MILLENNIAL HUMOR

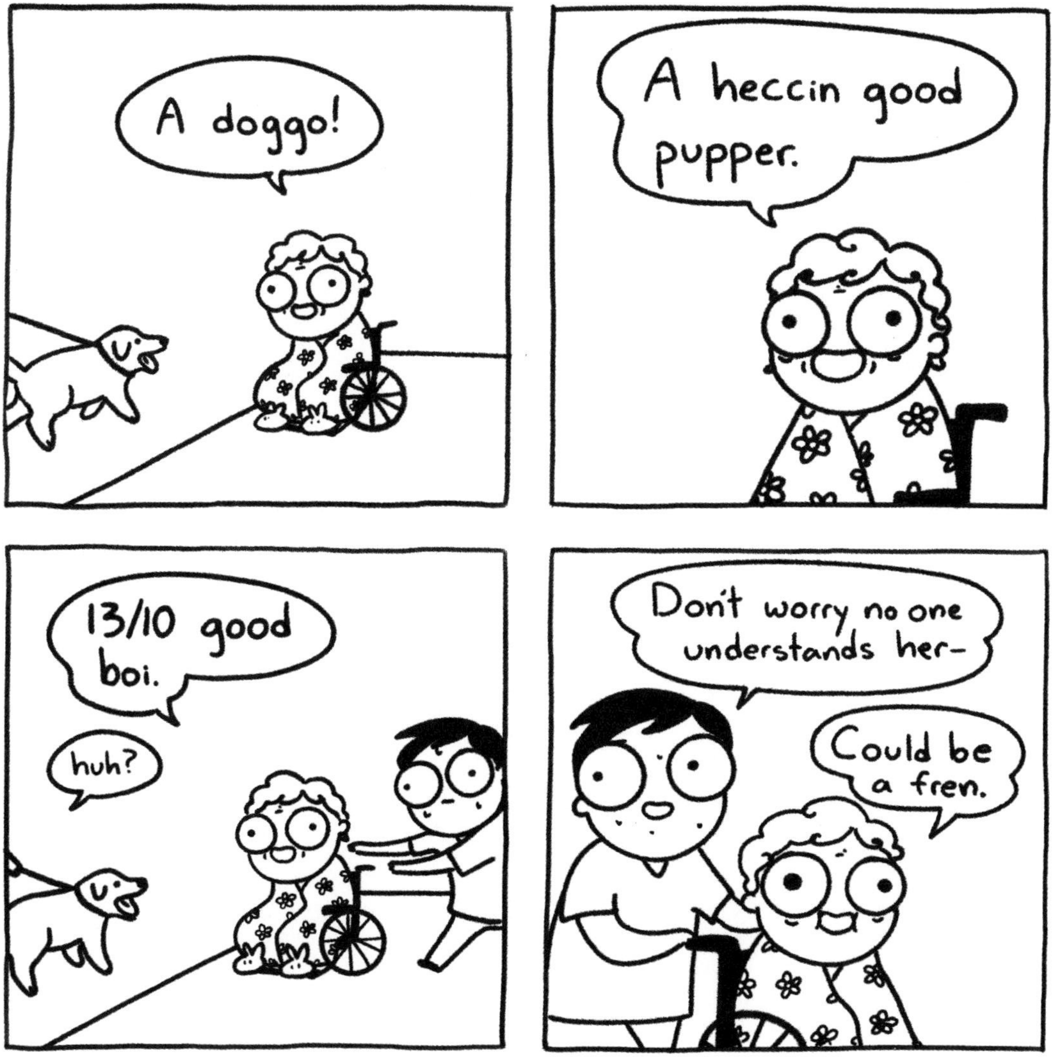
A doggo!
A heccin good pupper.
13/10 good boi.
huh?
Don't worry no one understands her-
Could be a fren.

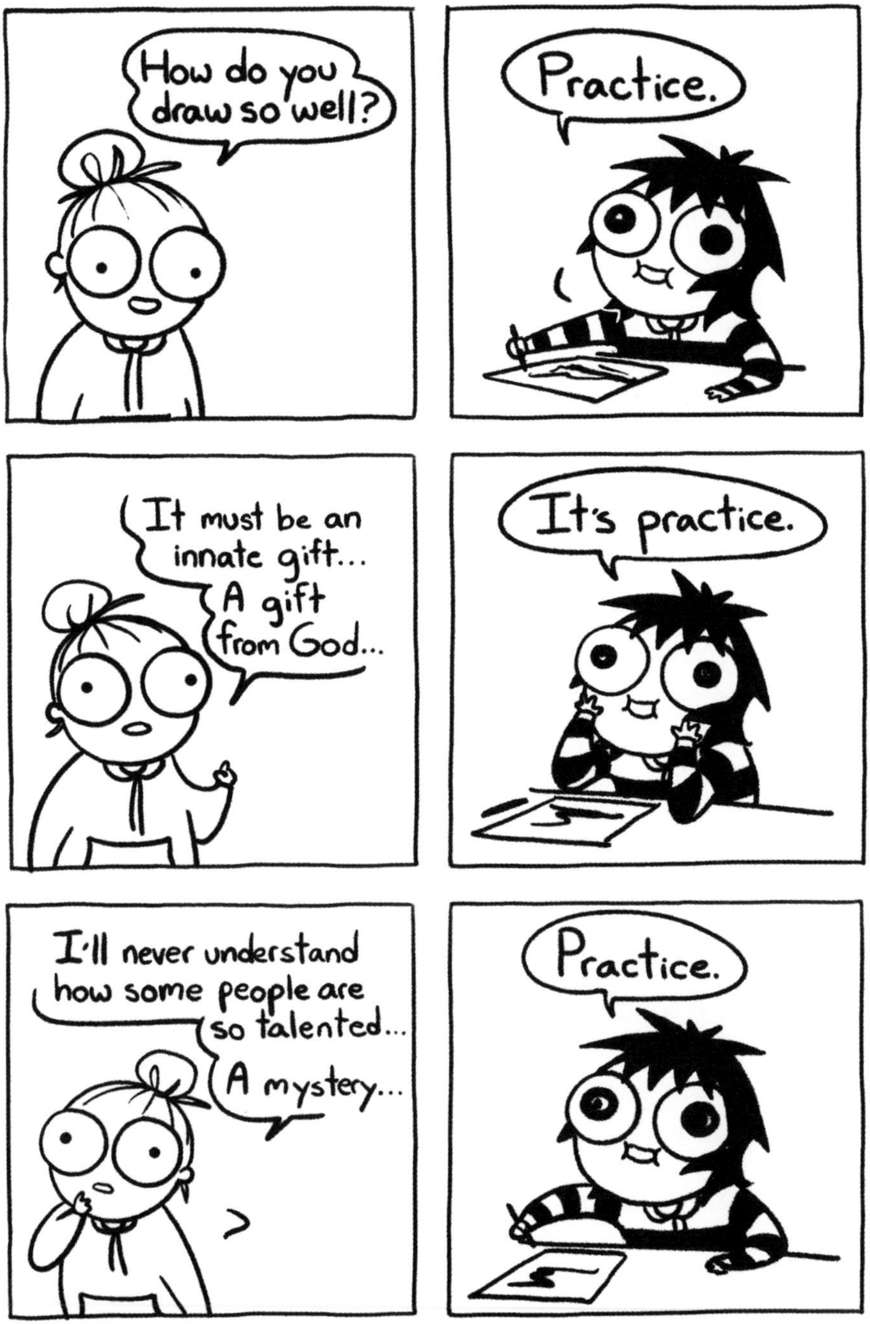
How do you draw so well?
Practice.
It must be an innate gift...
A gift from God...
It's practice.
I'll never understand how some people are so talented...
A mystery...
Practice.

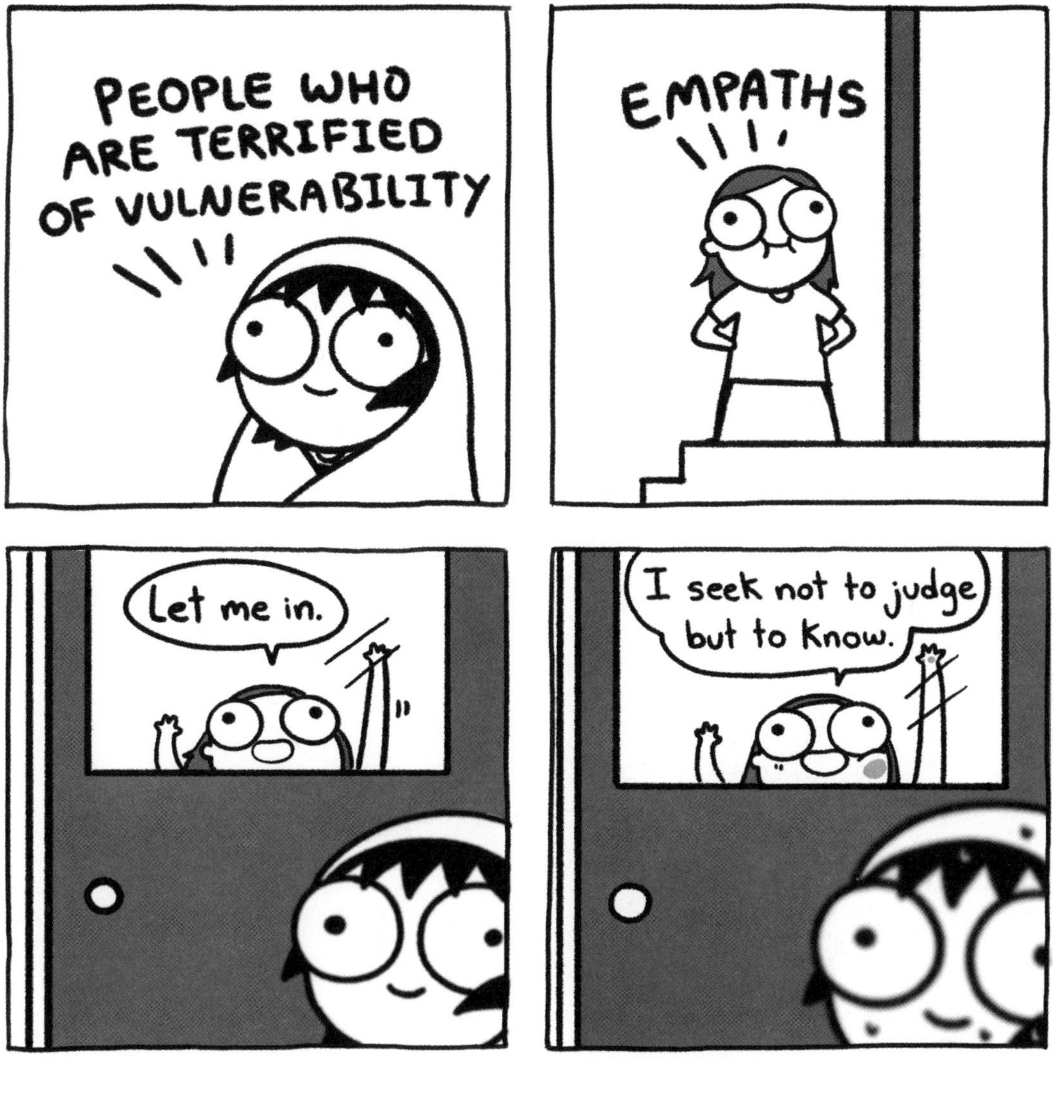
PEOPLE WHO ARE TERRIFIED OF VULNERABILITY
EMPATHS
Let me in.
I seek not to judge but to know.

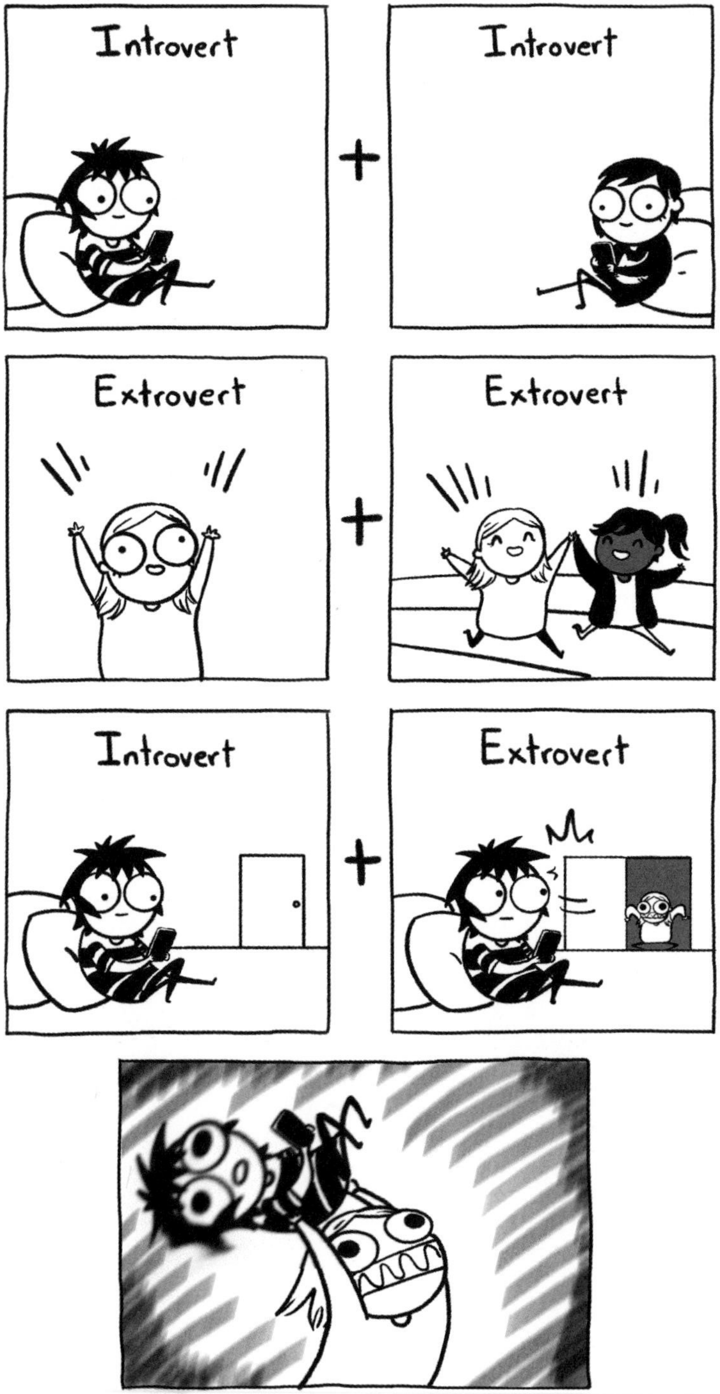
Introvert
Introvert
Extrovert
Extrovert
Introvert
Extrovert

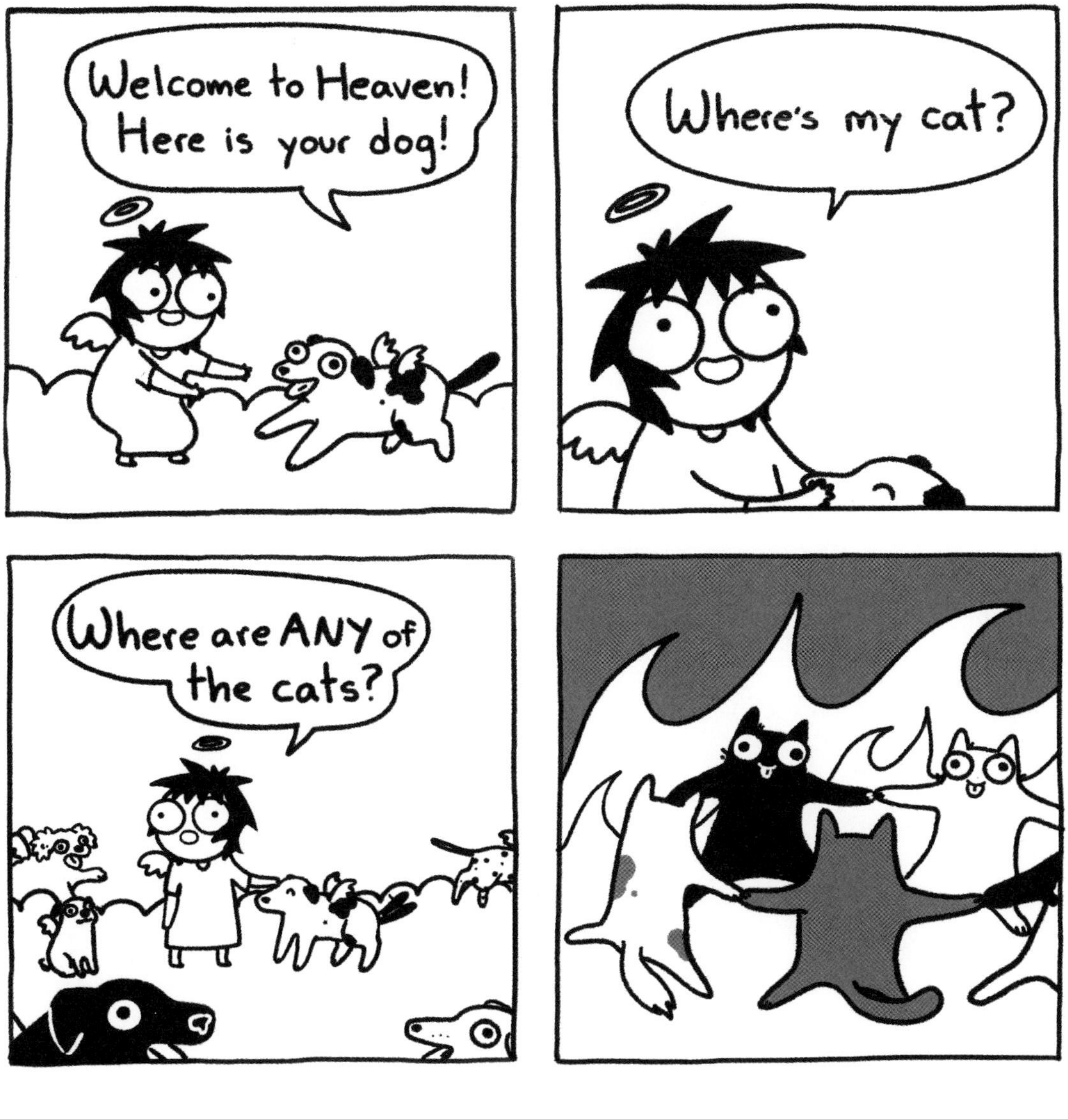
Welcome to Heaven! Here is your dog!
Where's my cat?
Where are ANY of the cats?

MILLENNIALS AS TEENS

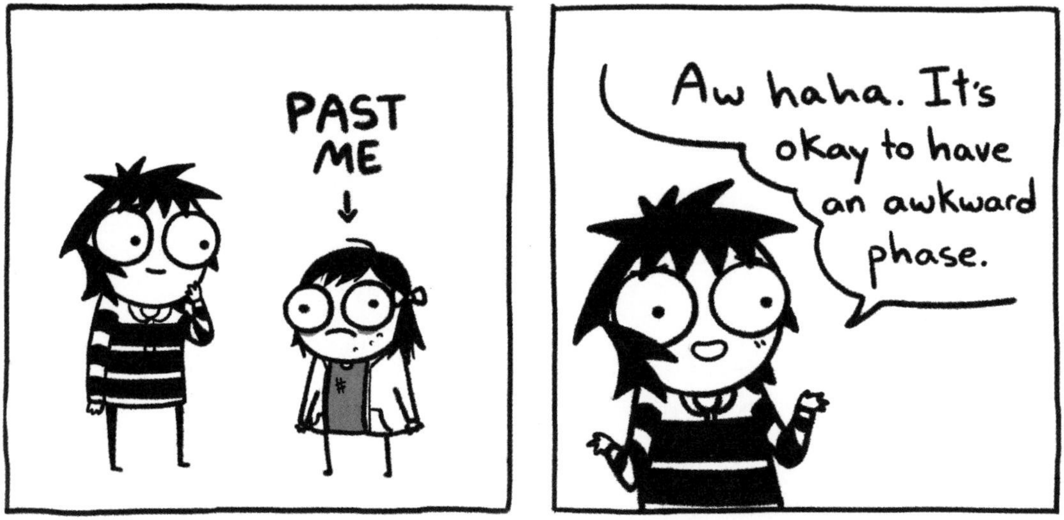
PAST
ME
Aw haha. It's okay to have an awkward phase.

GEN Z AS TEENS

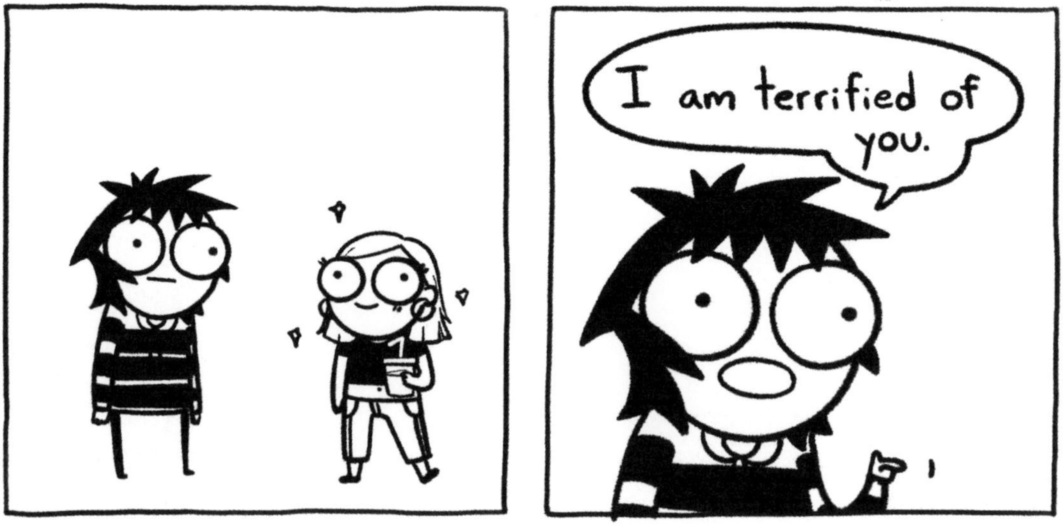
I am terrified of you.

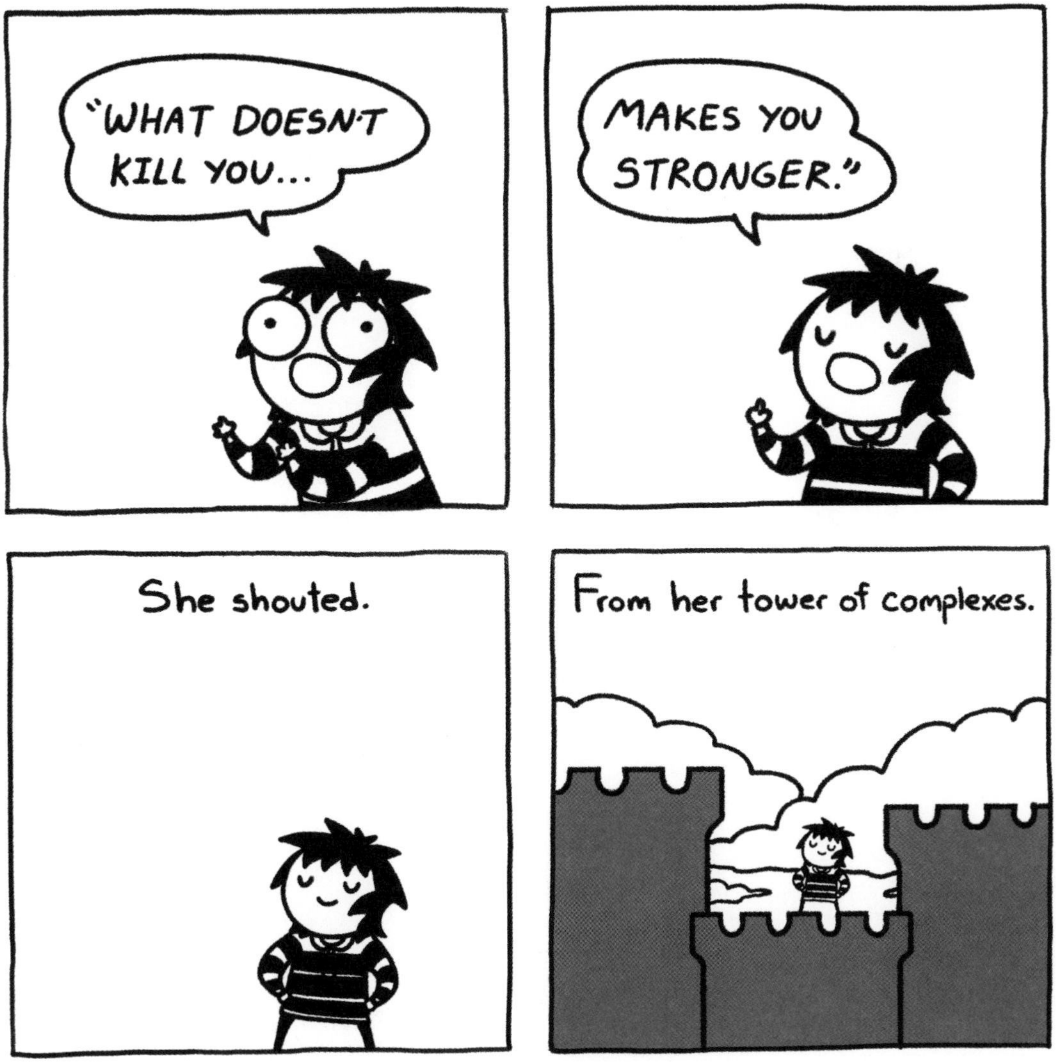
"WHAT DOESN'T KILL YOU...
MAKES YOU STRONGER."
She shouted.
From her tower of complexes.

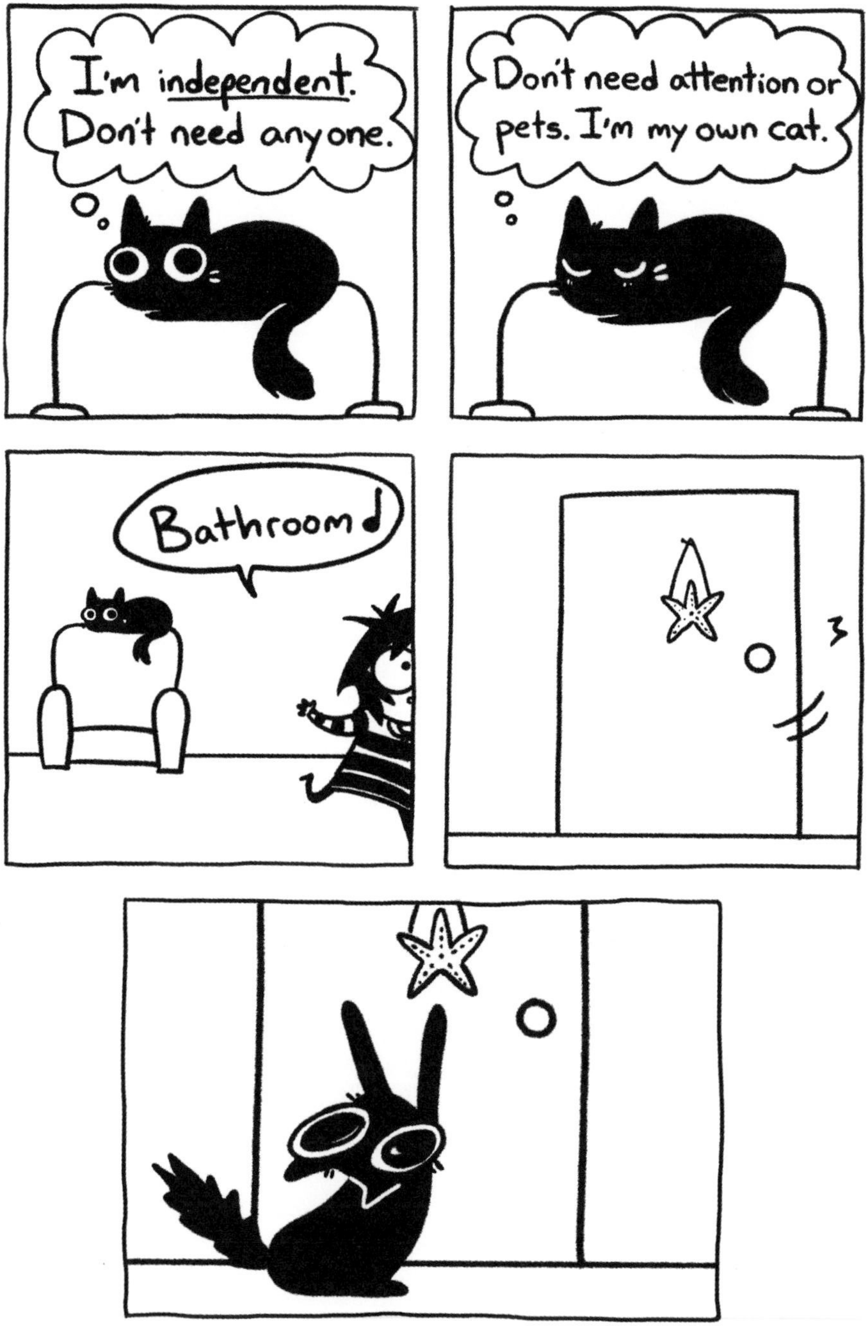
I'm independent. Don't need anyone.
Don't need attention or pets. I'm my own cat.
Bathroom

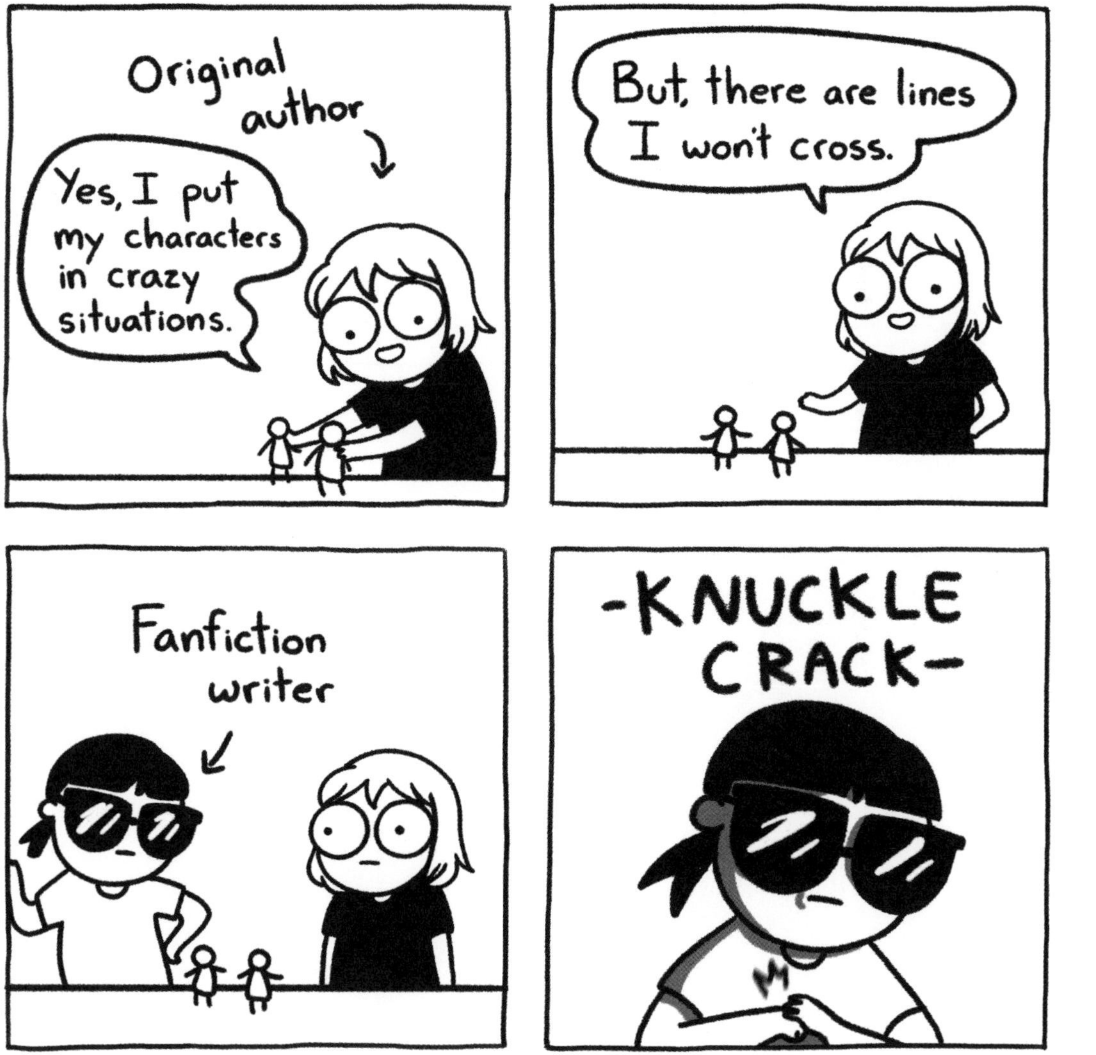
Original author
Yes, I put my characters in crazy situations.
But, there are lines I won't cross.
Fanfiction writer
-KNUCKLE CRACK-

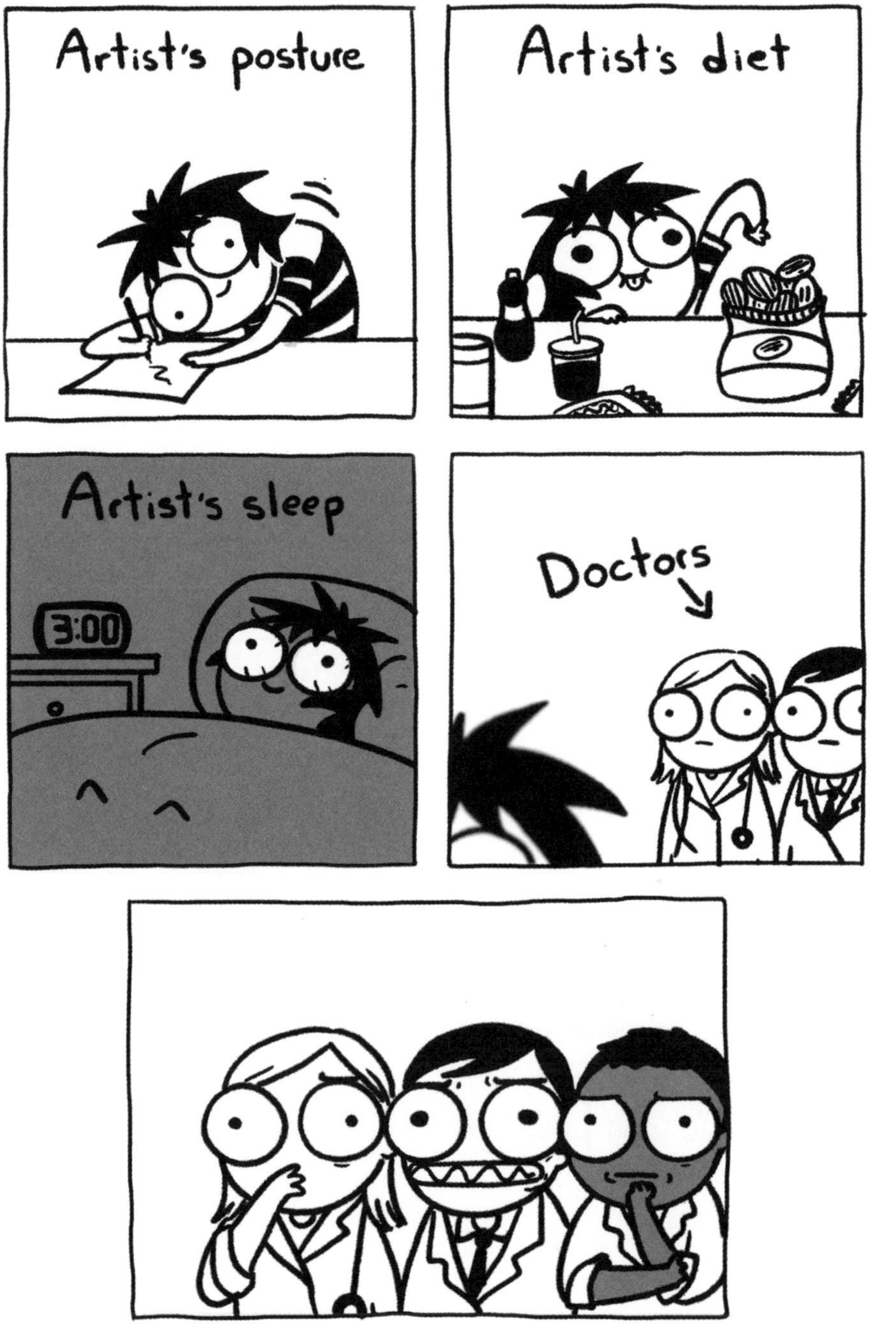
Artist's posture
Artist's diet
Artist's sleep
3:00
Doctors

GETTING INTO A SERIES YEARS TOO LATE

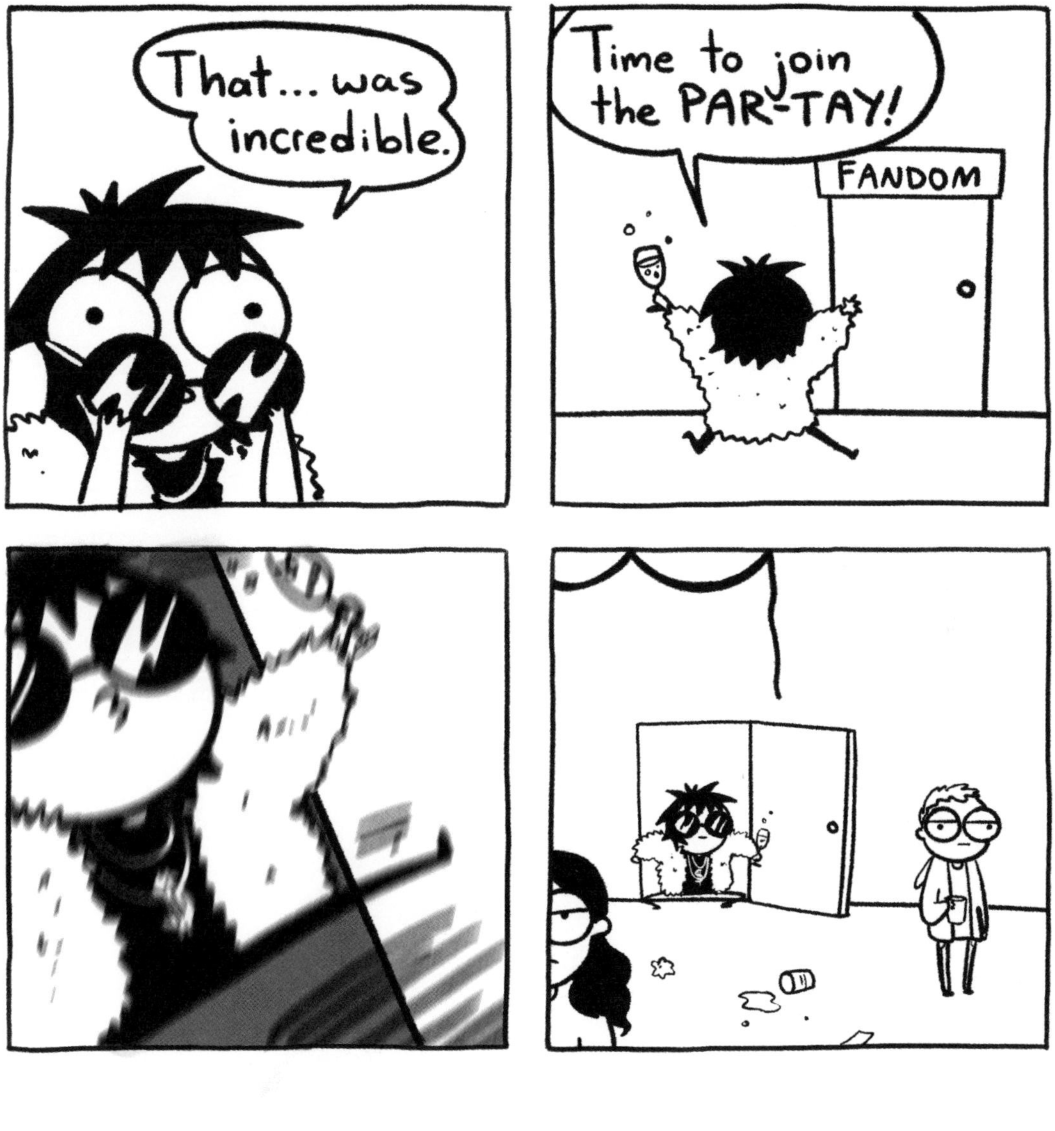
That... was incredible.
Time to join the PAR-TAY!
FANDOM

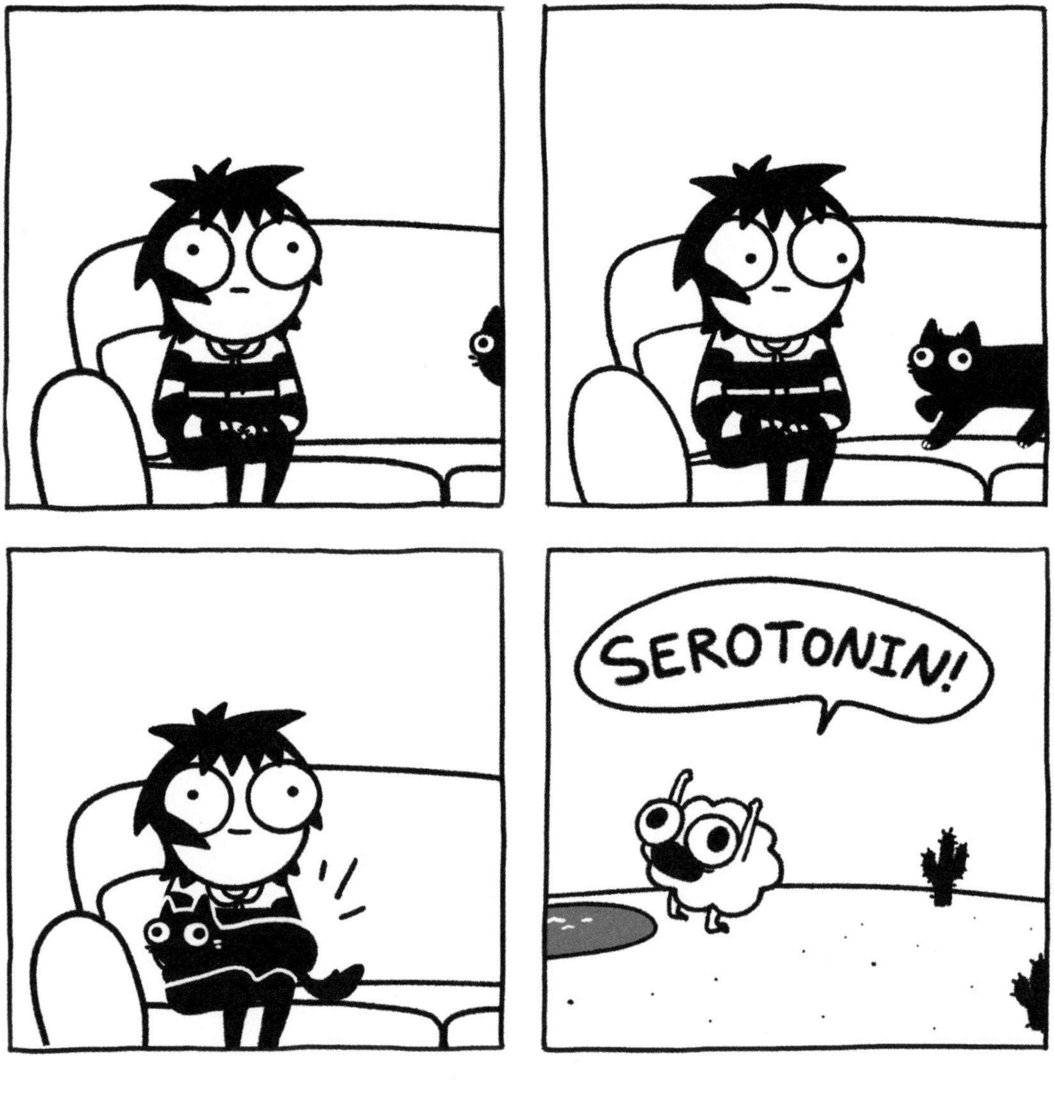
SEROTONIN!

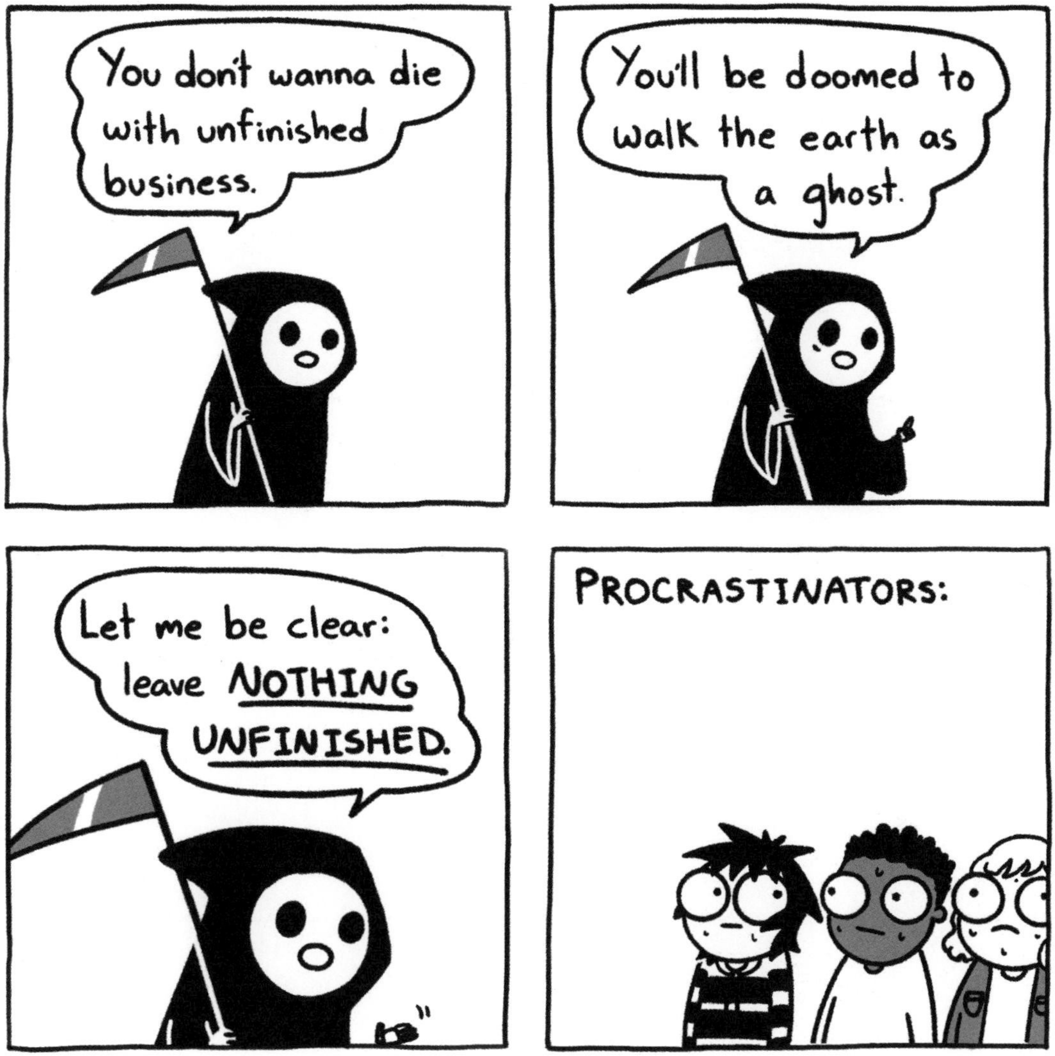
You don't wanna die with unfinished business.
You'll be doomed to walk the earth as a ghost.
Let me be clear: leave NOTHING UNFINISHED.
PROCRASTINATORS:

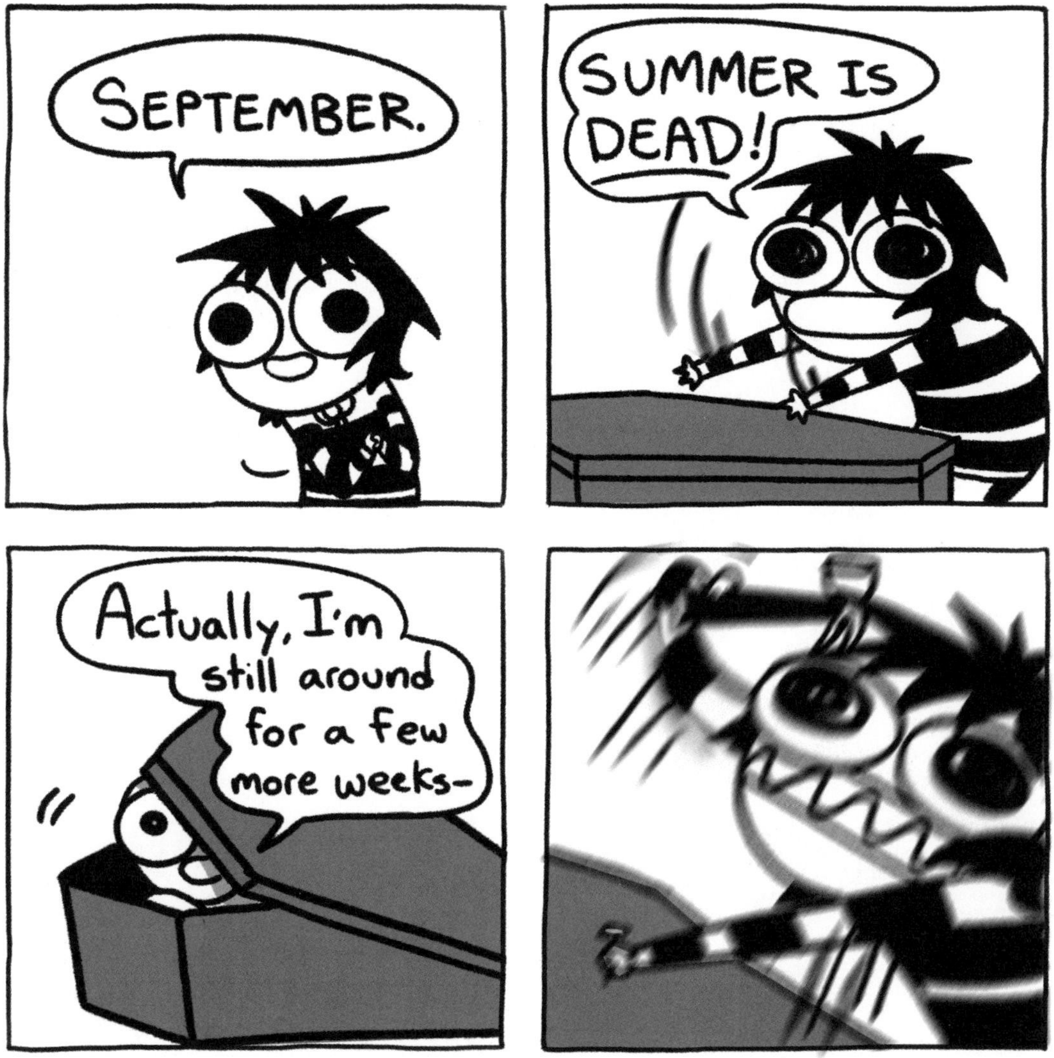
SEPTEMBER.
SUMMER IS DEAD!
Actually, I'm still around for a few more weeks-

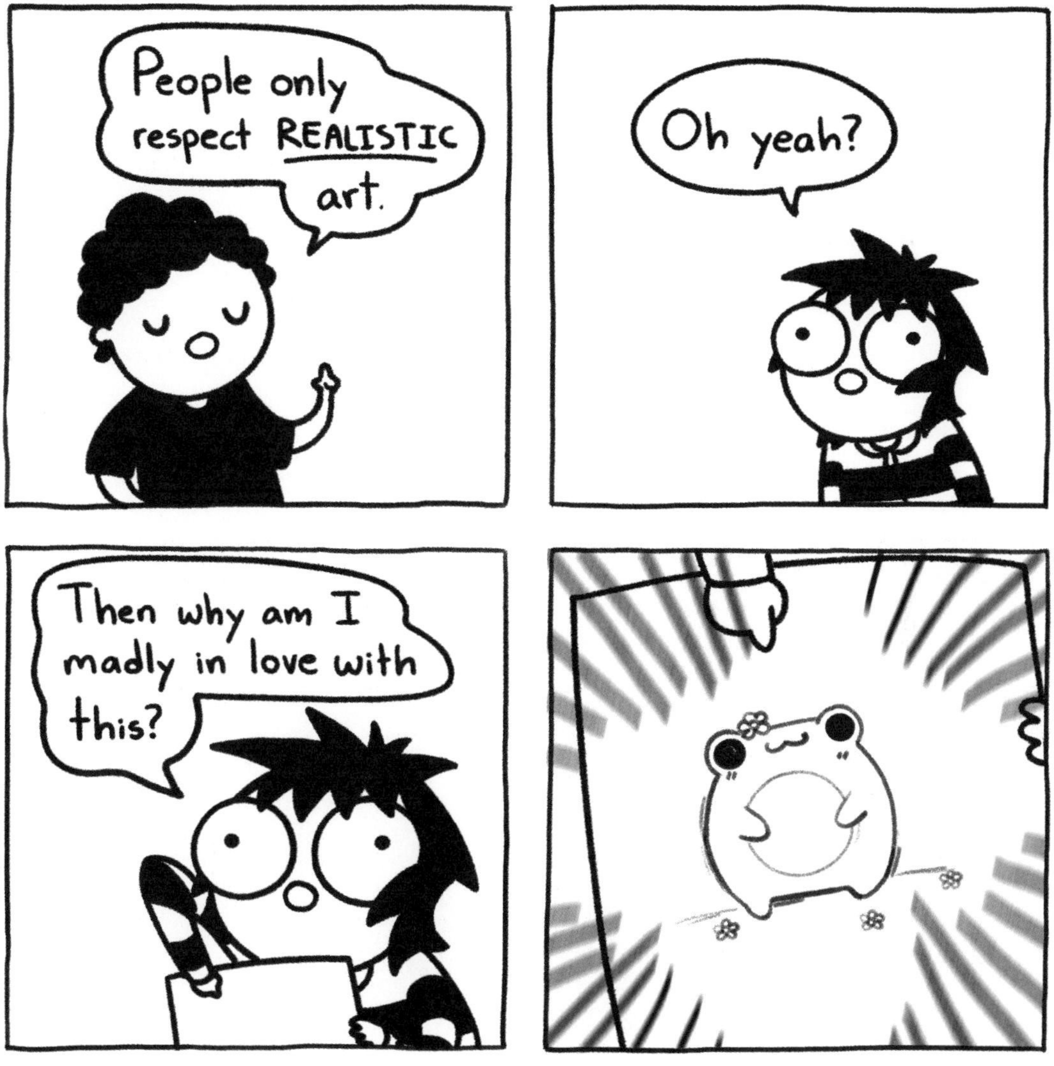
People only respect REALISTIC art.
Oh yeah?
Then why am I madly in love with this?

HALLOWEEN

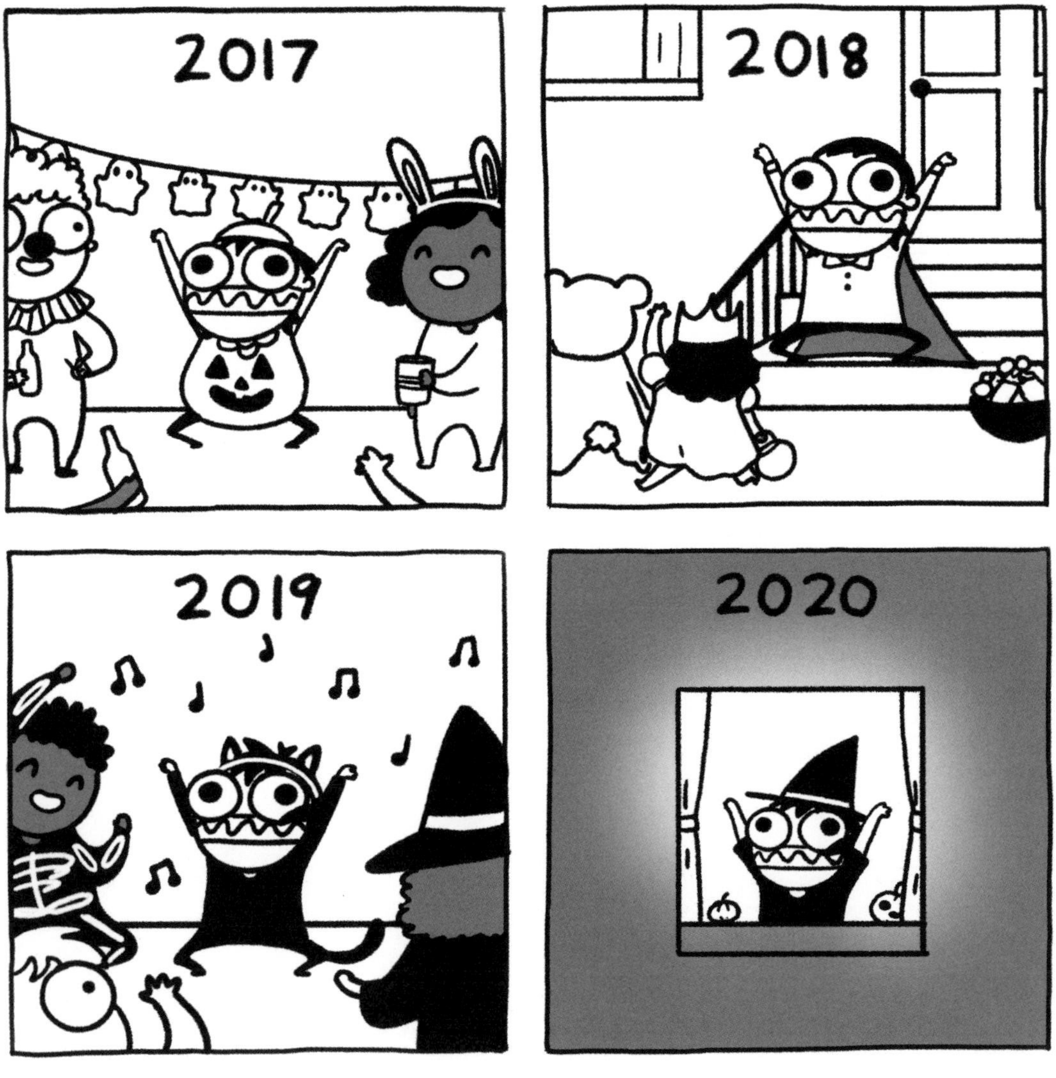
2017
2018
2019
2020

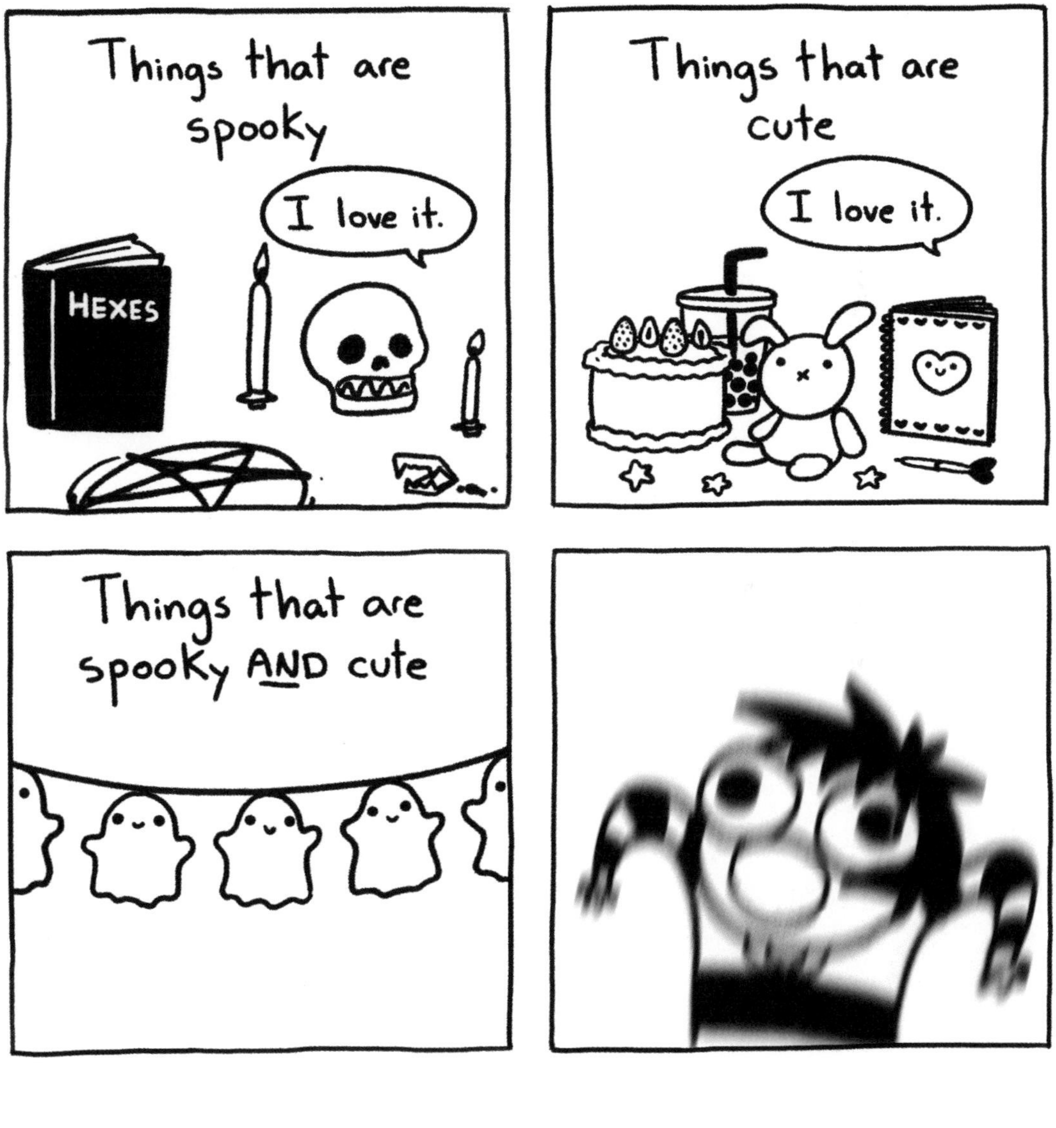
Things that are spooky
HEXES
I love it.
Things that are cute
I love it.
Things that are spooky AND cute

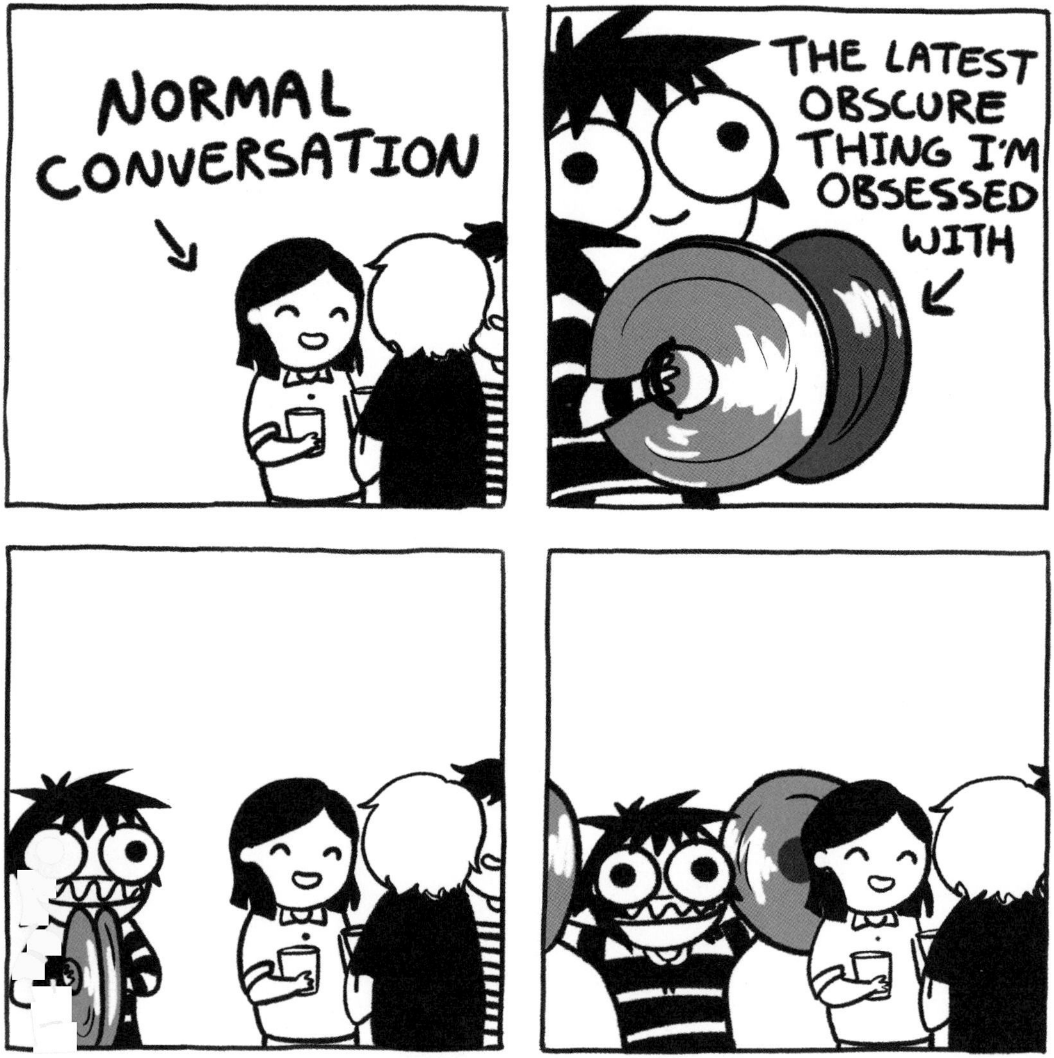
NORMAL CONVERSATION
THE LATEST OBSCURE THING I'M OBSESSED WITH

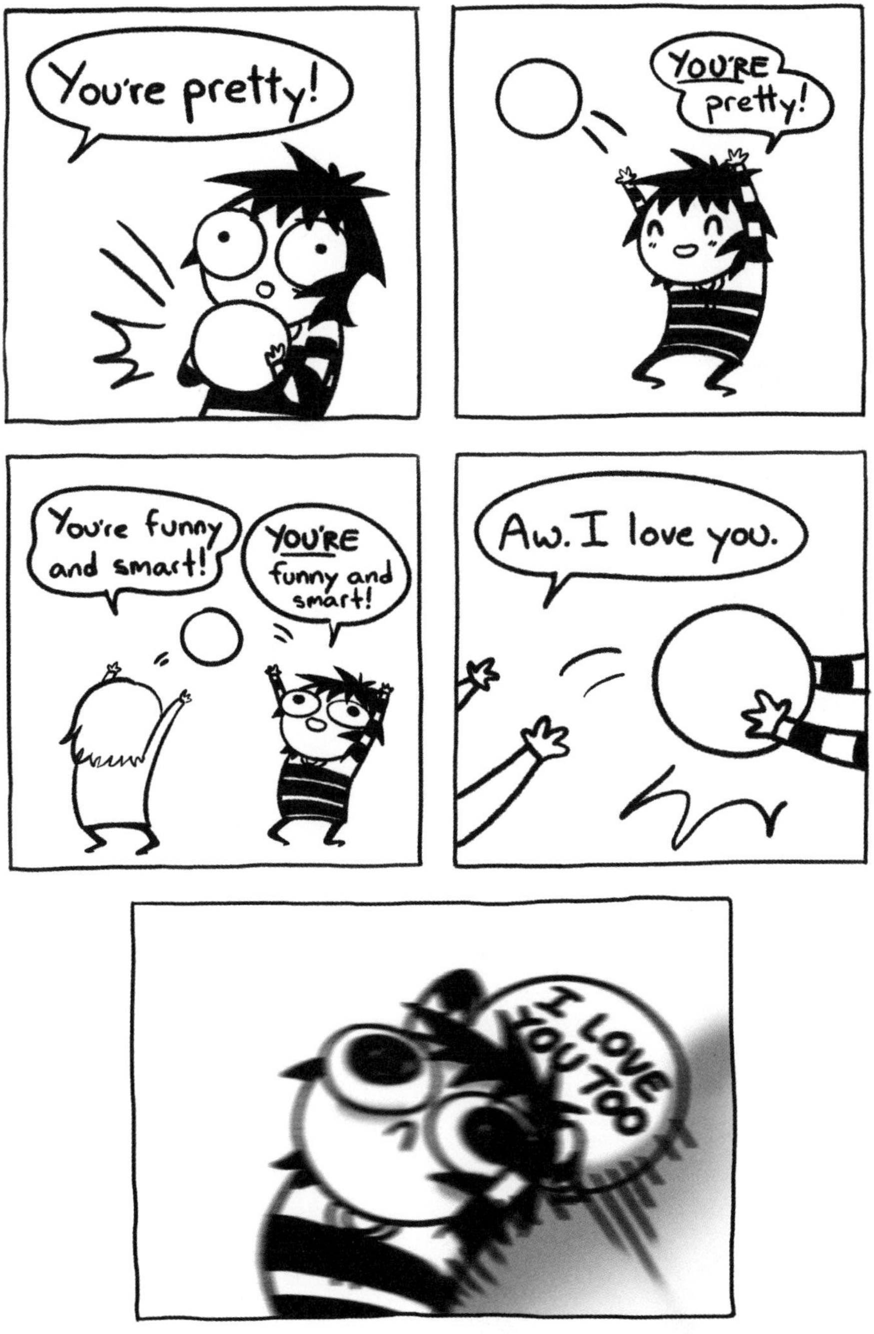
You're pretty!
YOU'RE pretty!
You're funny and smart!
YOU'RE funny and smart!
Aw. I love you.
I LOVE YOU TOO

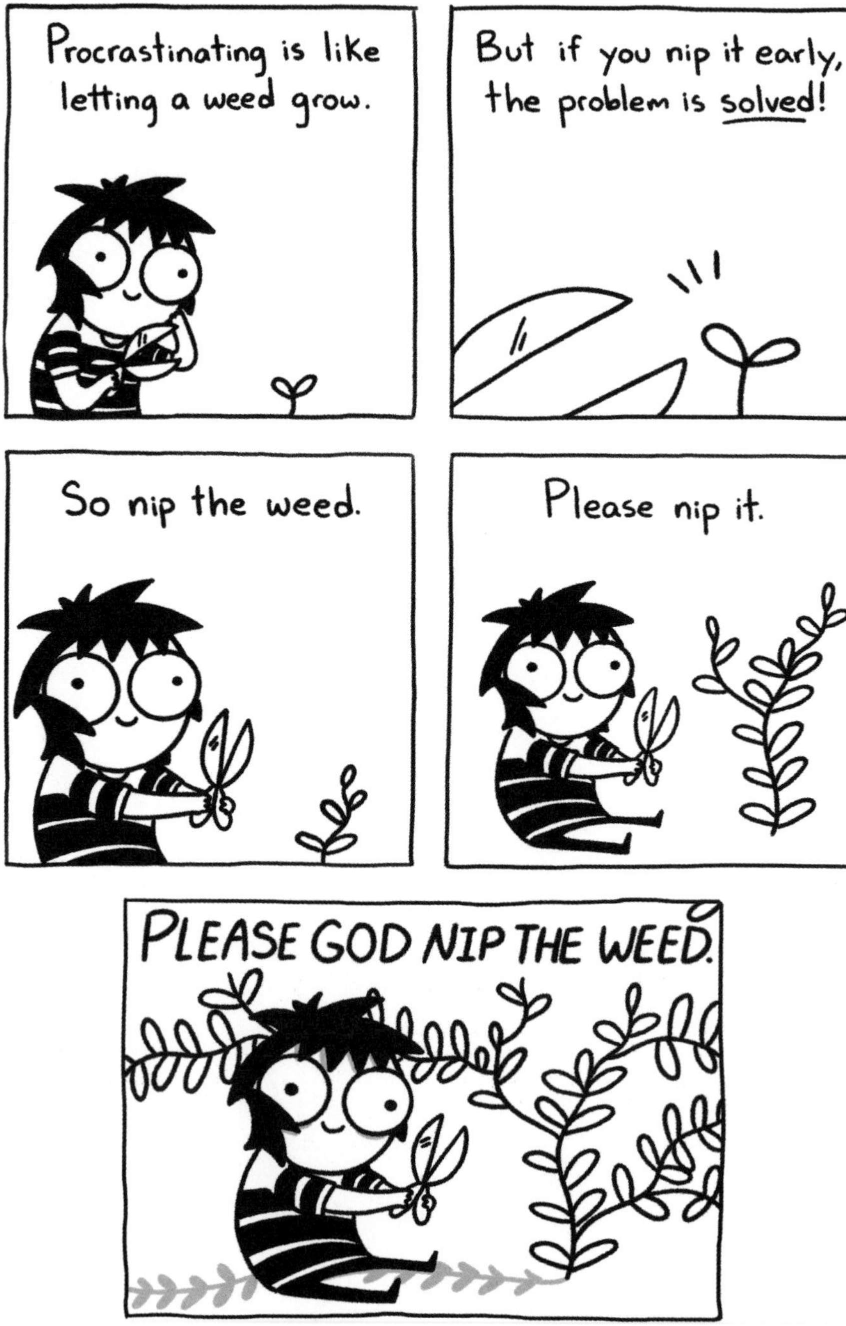
Procrastinating is like letting a weed grow.
But if you nip it early, the problem is solved!
So nip the weed.
Please nip it.
PLEASE GOD NIP THE WEED.

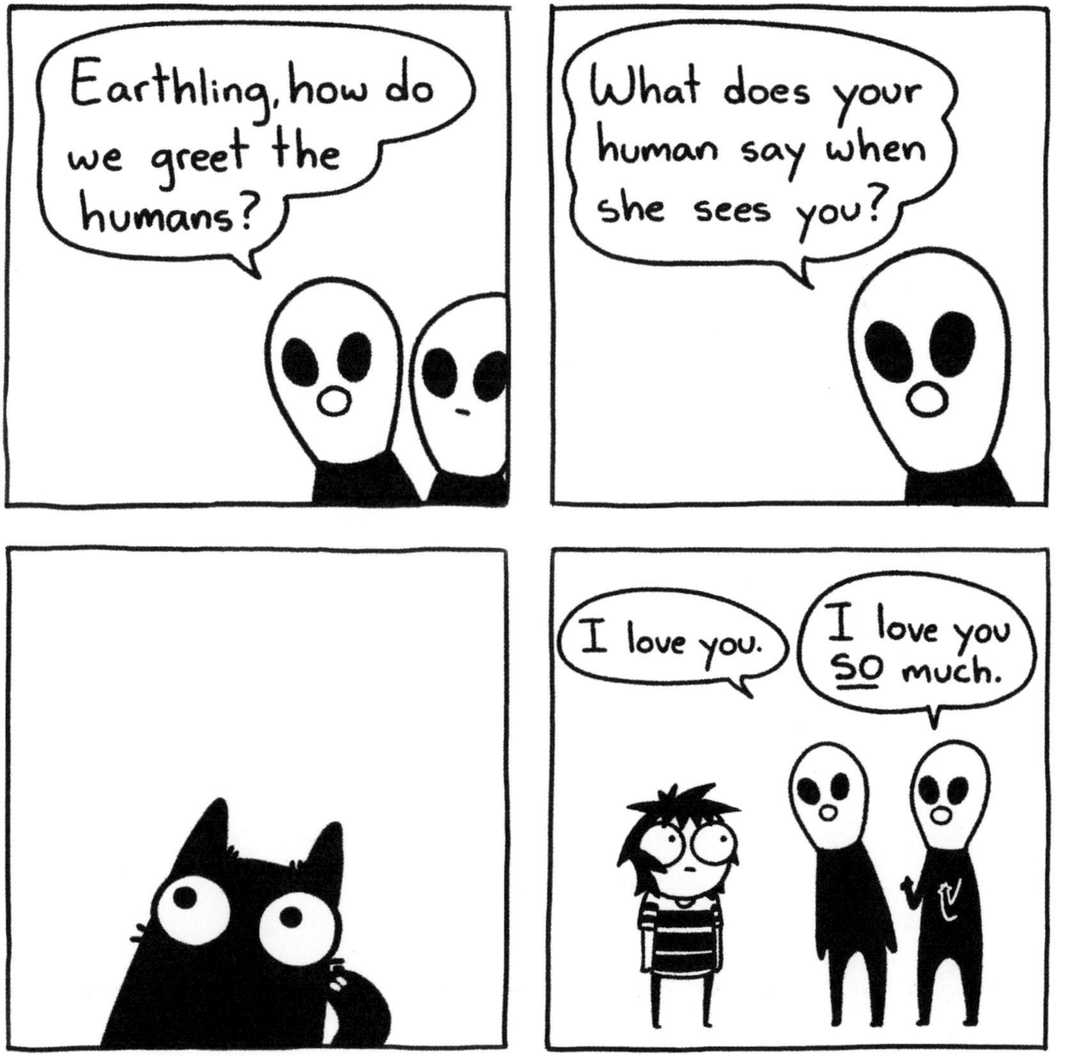
Earthling, how do we greet the humans?
What does your human say when she sees you?
I love you.
I love you SO much.

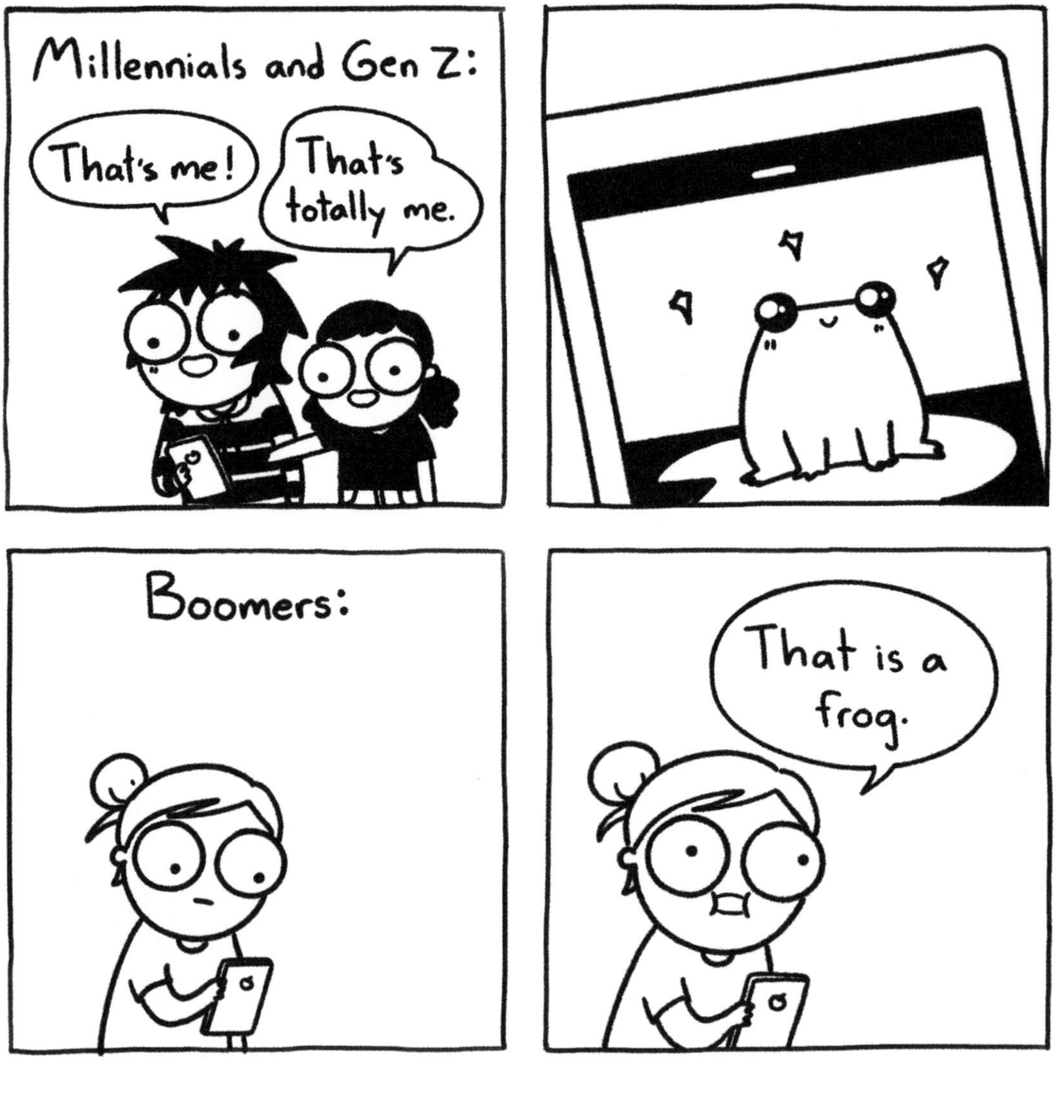
Millennials and Gen Z:
That's me!
That's totally me.
Boomers:
That is a frog.

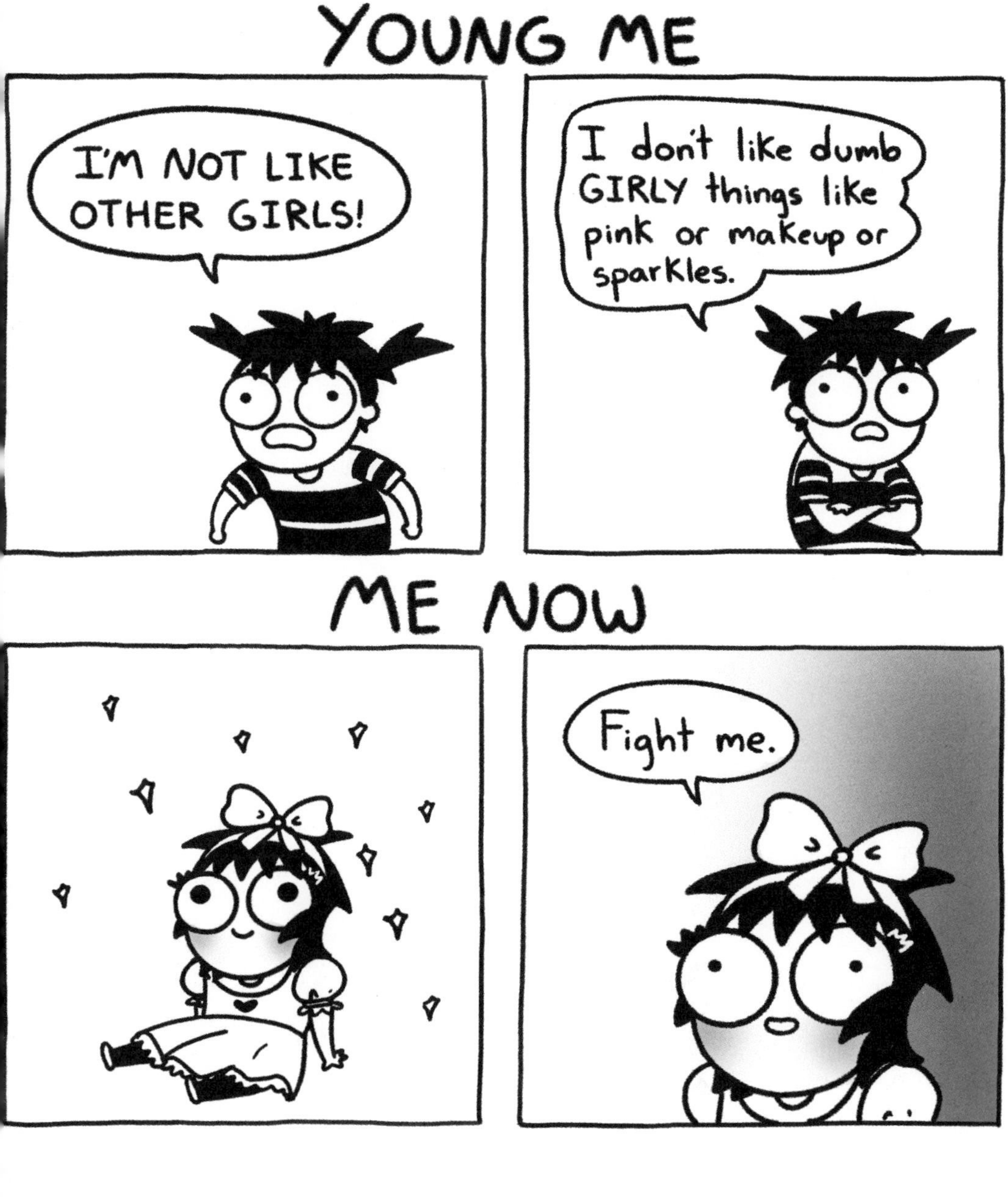
YOUNG ME
I'M NOT LIKE OTHER GIRLS!
I don't like dumb GIRLY things like pink or makeup or sparkles.
ME NOW
Fight me.

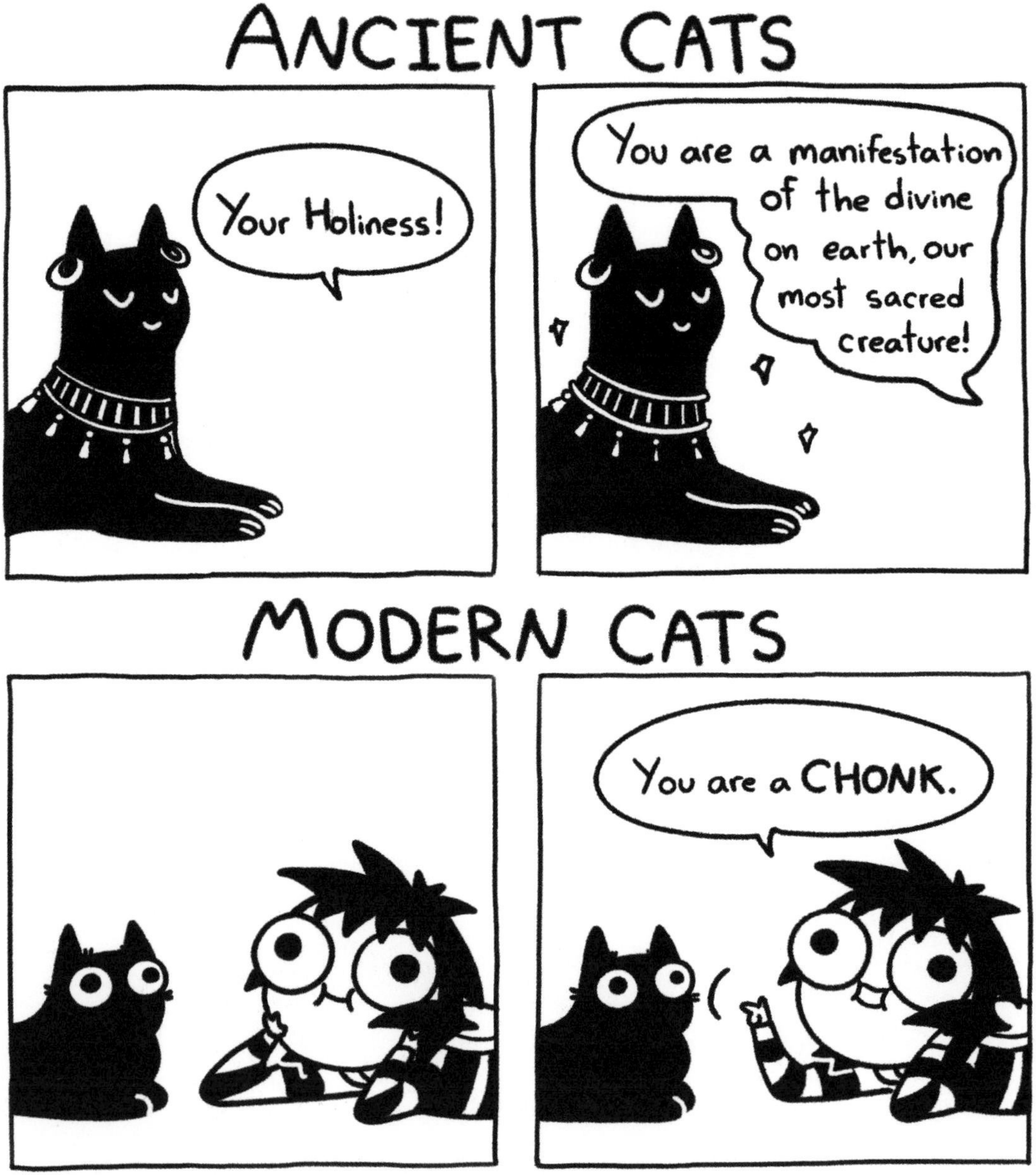
ANCIENT CATS
Your Holiness!
You are a manifestation of the divine on earth, our most sacred creature!
MODERN CATS
You are a CHONK.

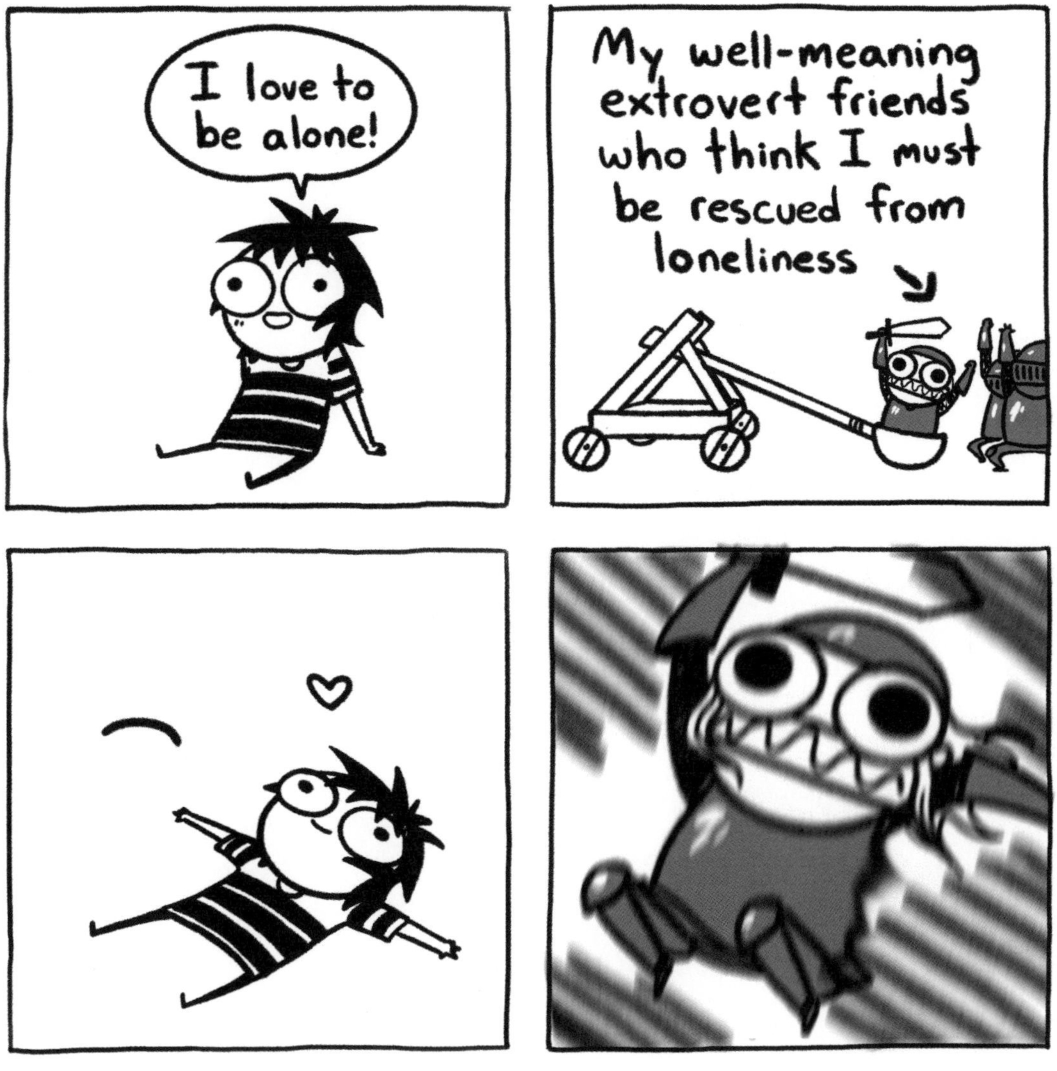
I love to be alone!
My well-meaning extrovert friends who think I must be rescued from loneliness

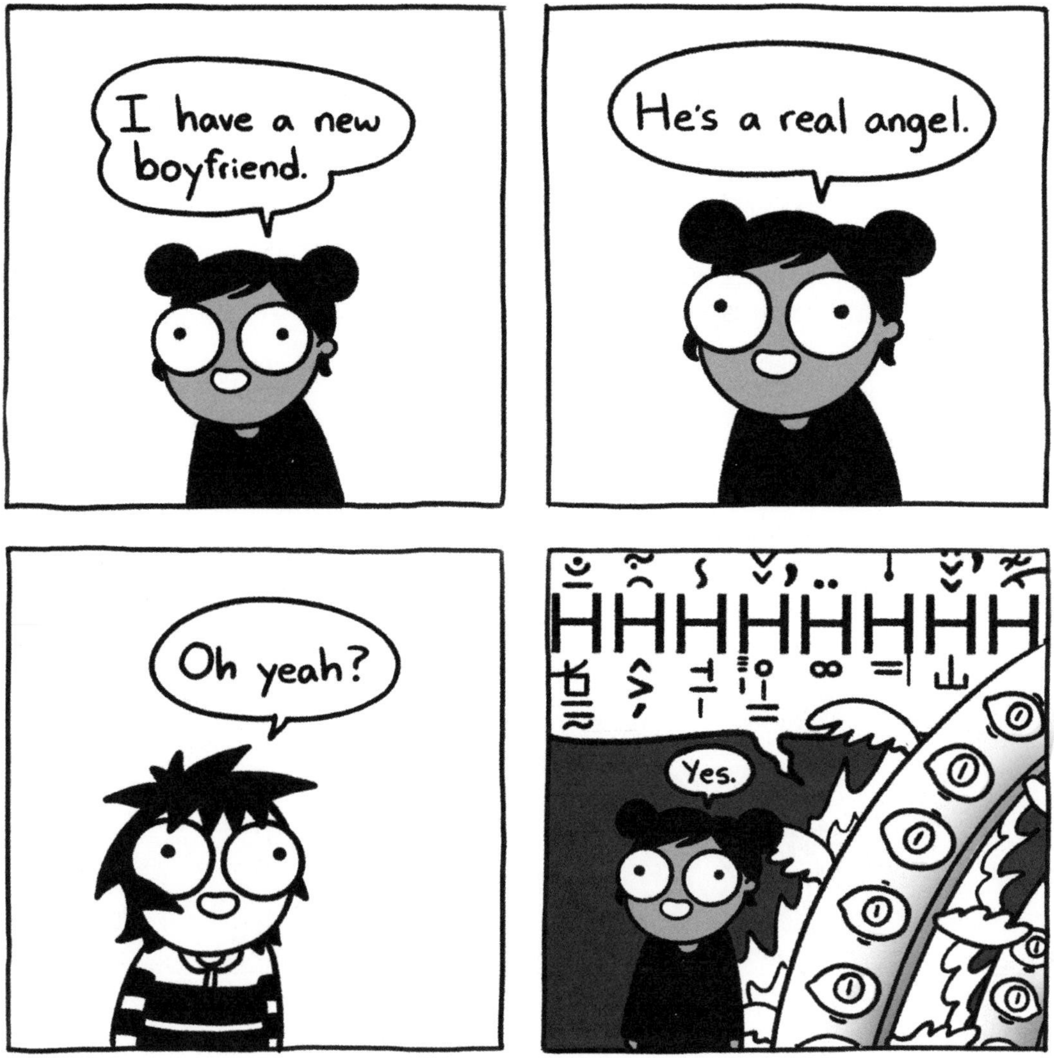
I have a new boyfriend.
He's a real angel.
Oh yeah?
HHHHHHHH
Yes.

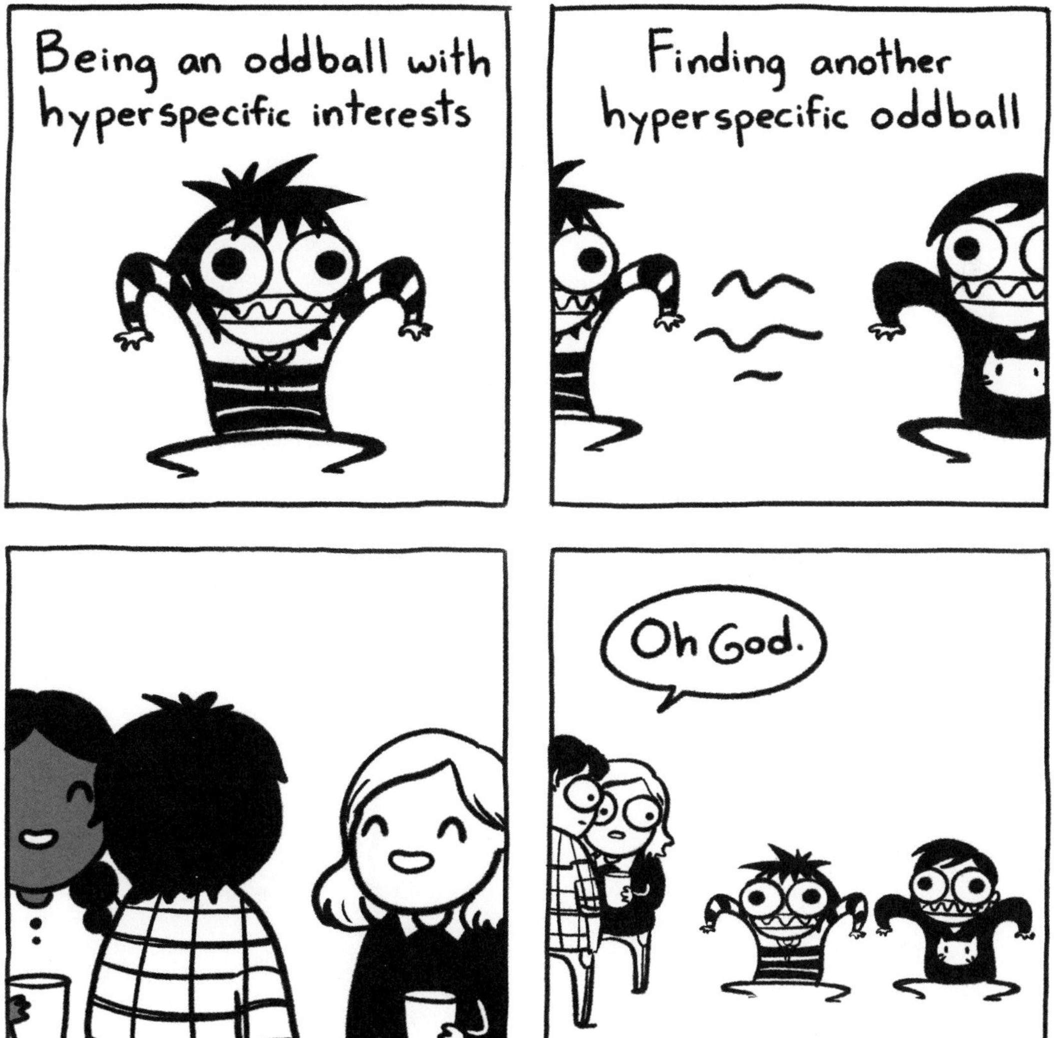
Being an oddball with hyperspecific interests
Finding another hyperspecific oddball
Oh God.

TIME TRAVELING

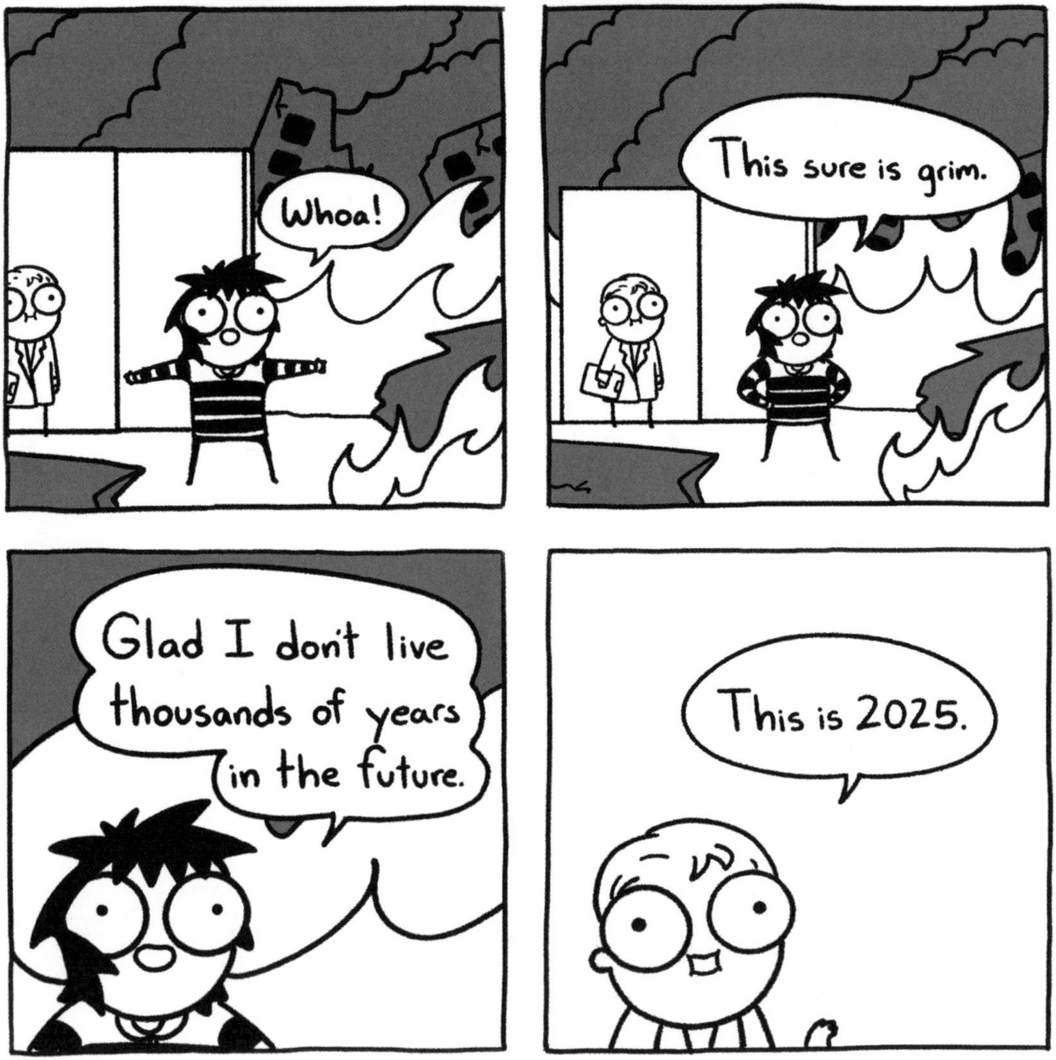
Whoa!
This sure is grim.
Glad I don't live thousands of years in the future.
This is 2025.

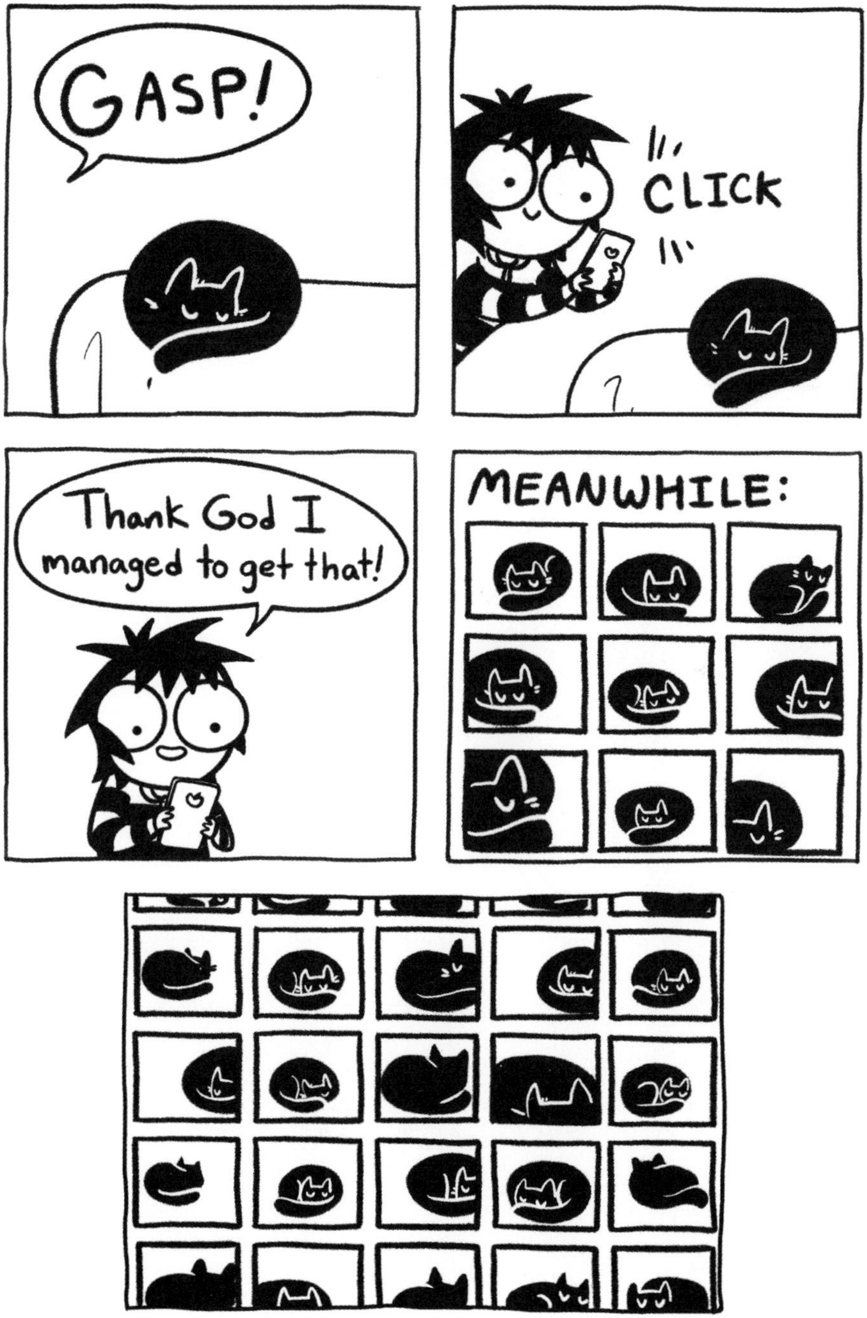
GASP!
CLICK
Thank God I managed to get that!
MEANWHILE:

ANXIOUS FRIENDS

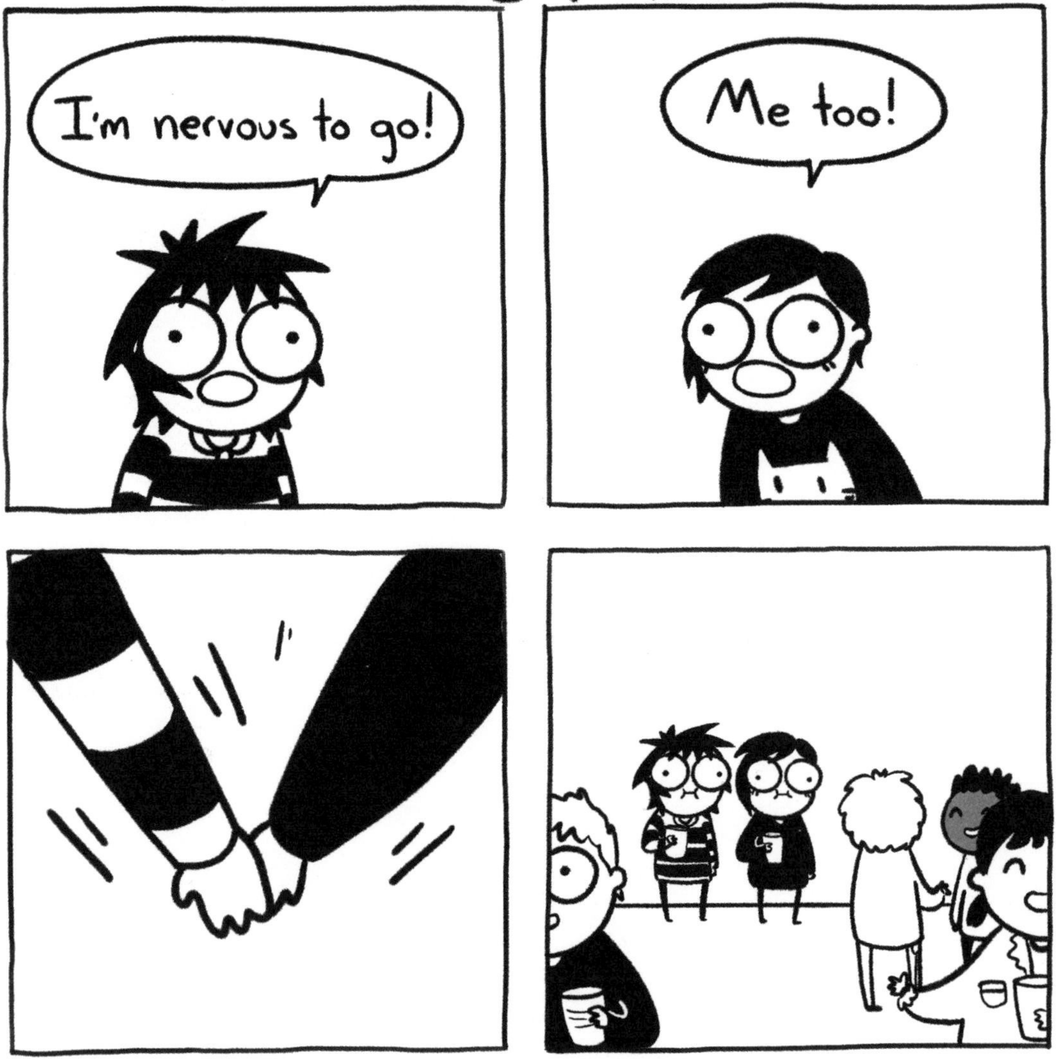

I'm nervous to go!
Me too!

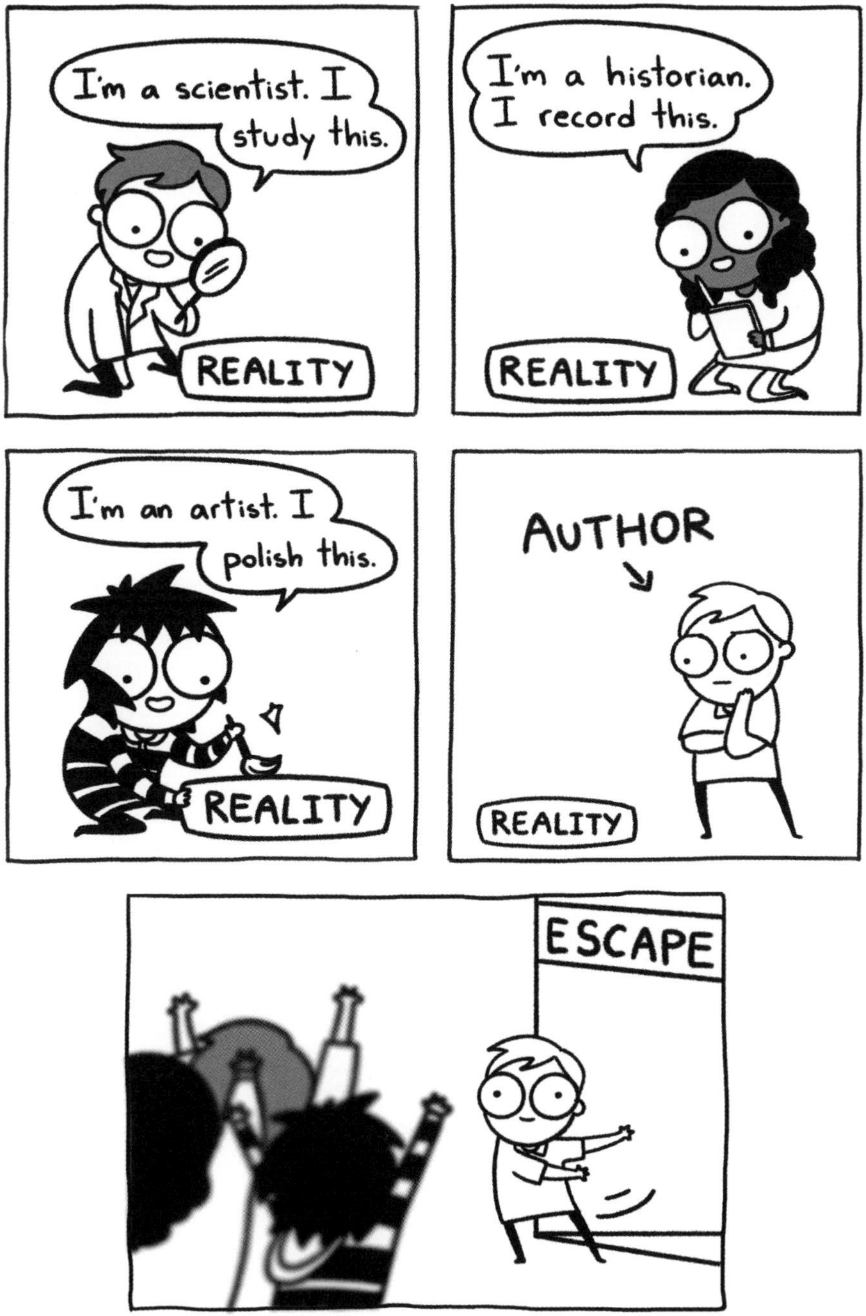
I'm a scientist. I study this.
REALITY
I'm a historian. I record this.
REALITY
I'm an artist. I polish this.
REALITY
AUTHOR
REALITY
ESCAPE

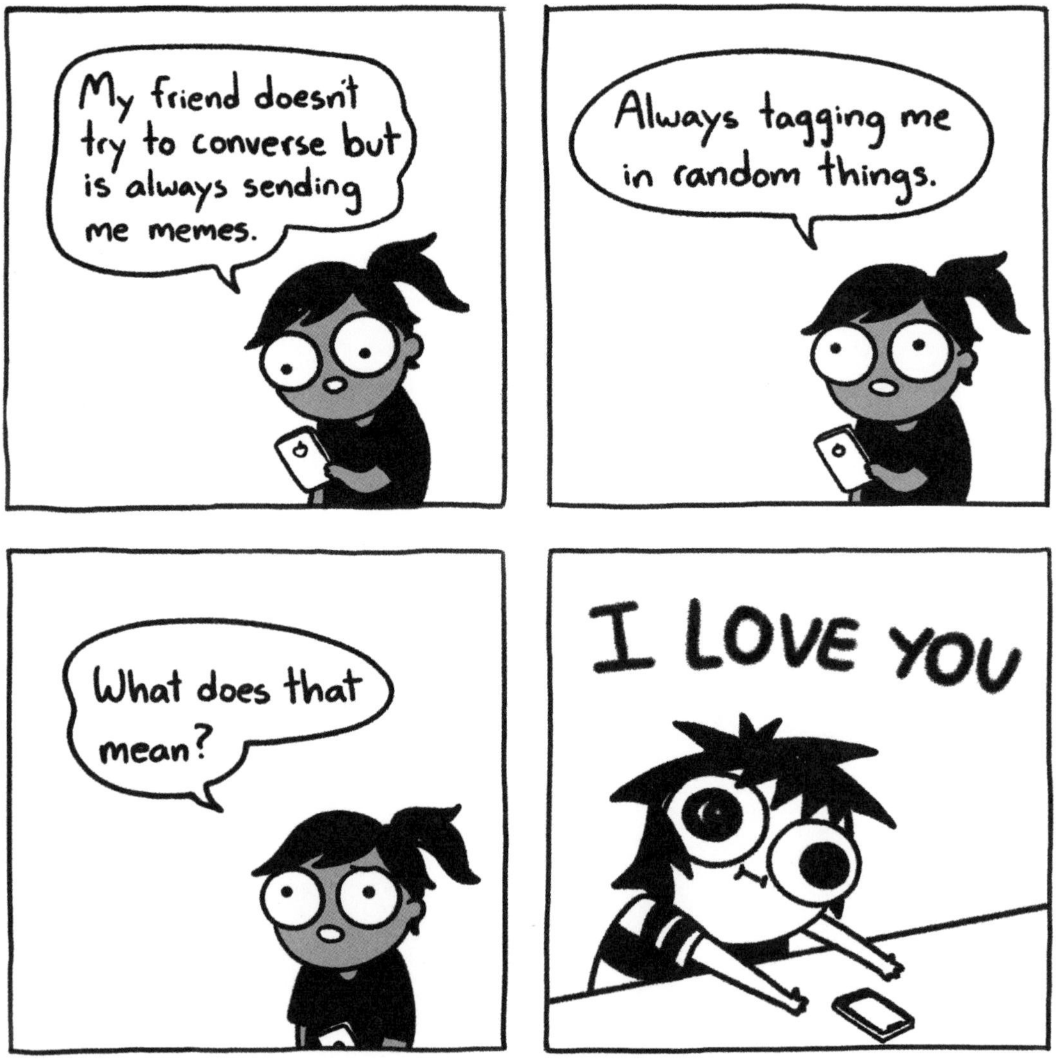
My friend doesn't try to converse but is always sending me memes.
Always tagging me in random things.
What does that mean?
I LOVE YOU

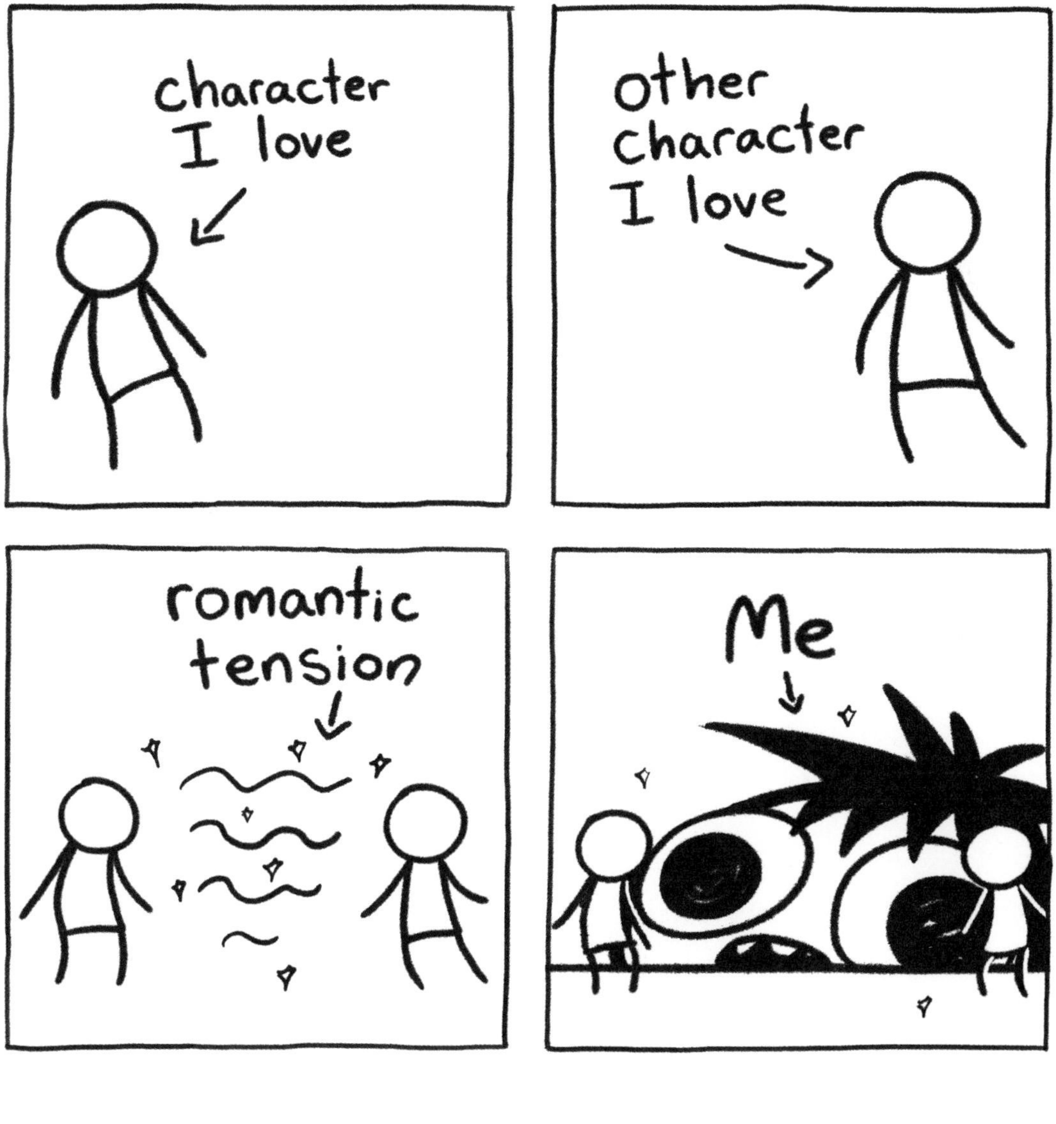
character I love
other character I love
romantic tension
Me

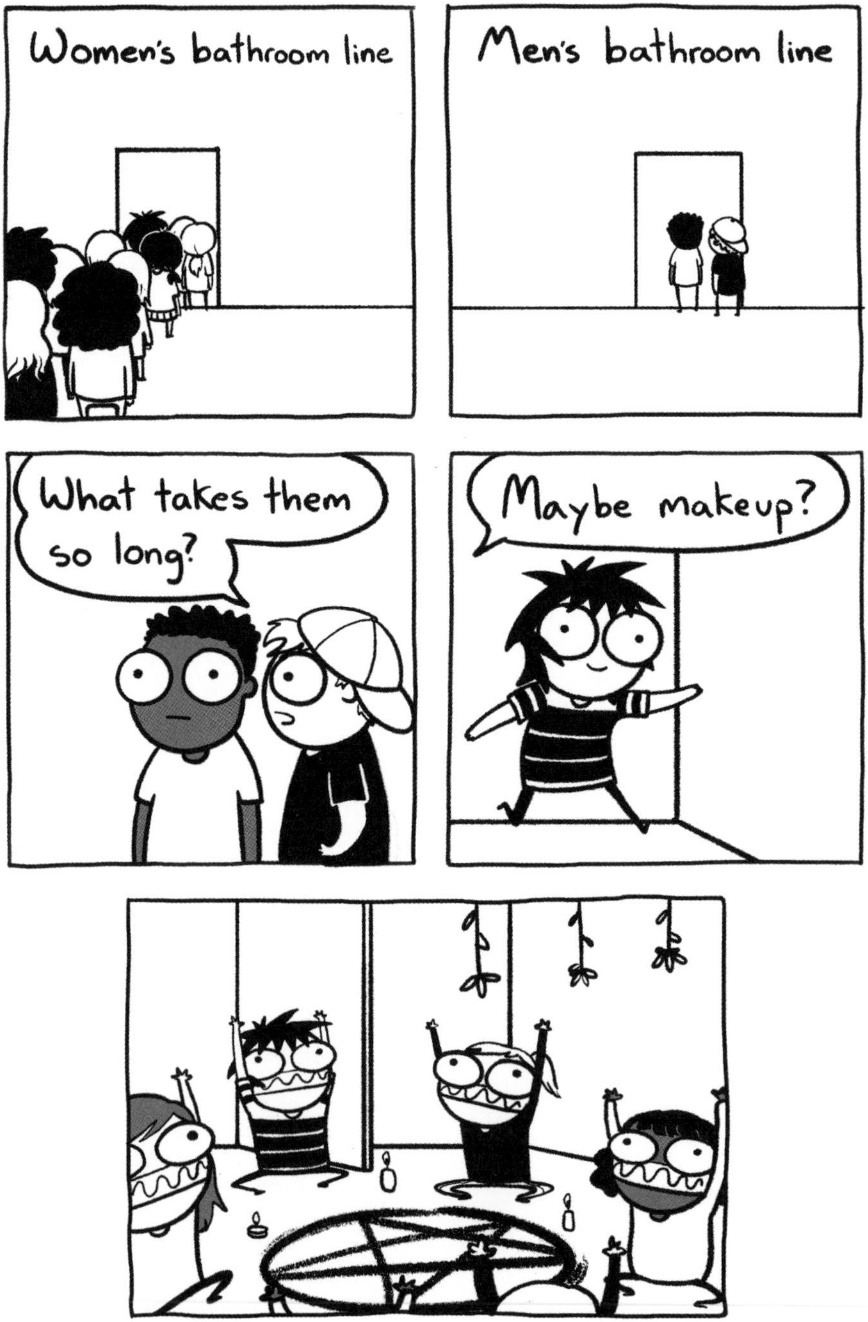
Women's bathroom line
Men's bathroom line
What takes them so long?
Maybe makeup?

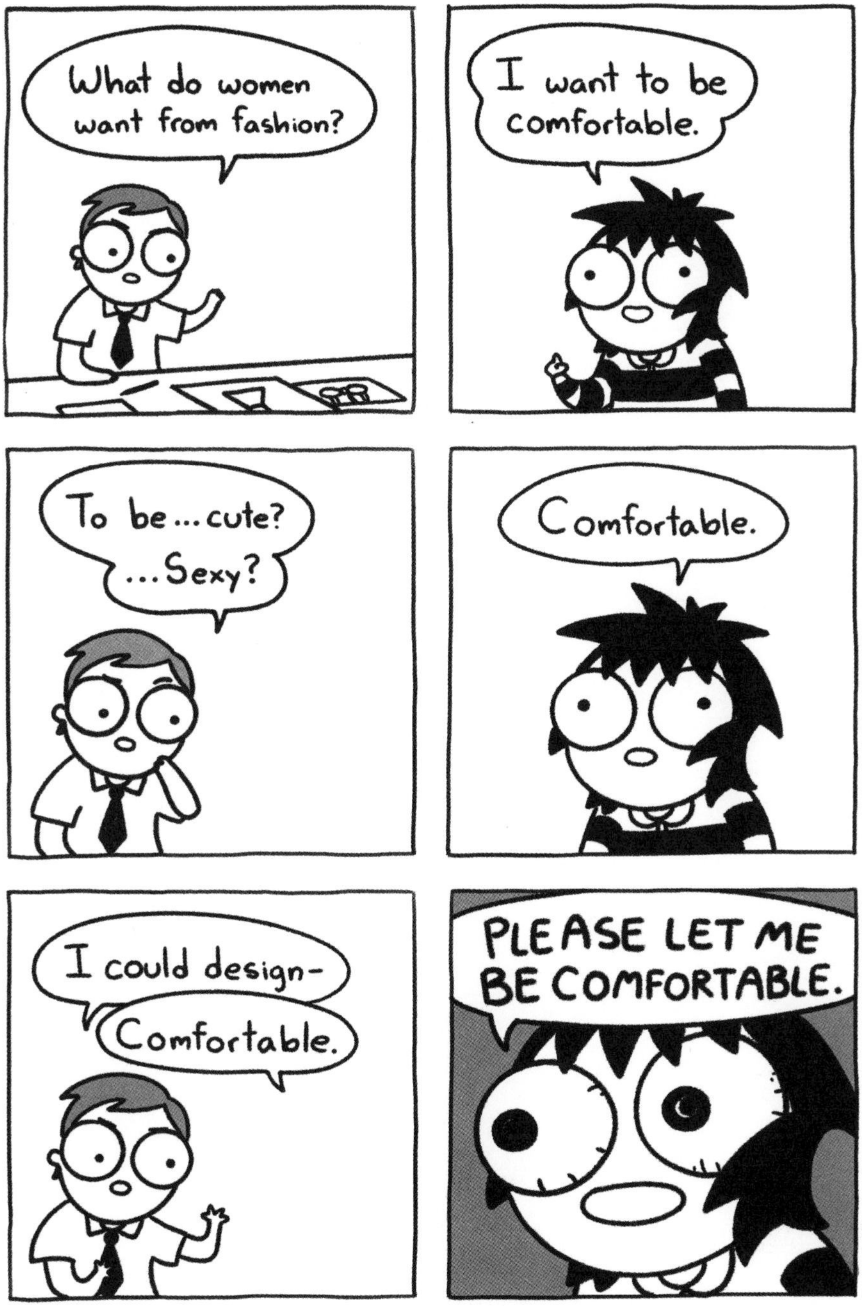
What do women want from fashion?
I want to be comfortable.
To be...cute?
...Sexy?
Comfortable.
I could design-
Comfortable.
PLEASE LET ME BE COMFORTABLE.

ENJOYING SOMETHING

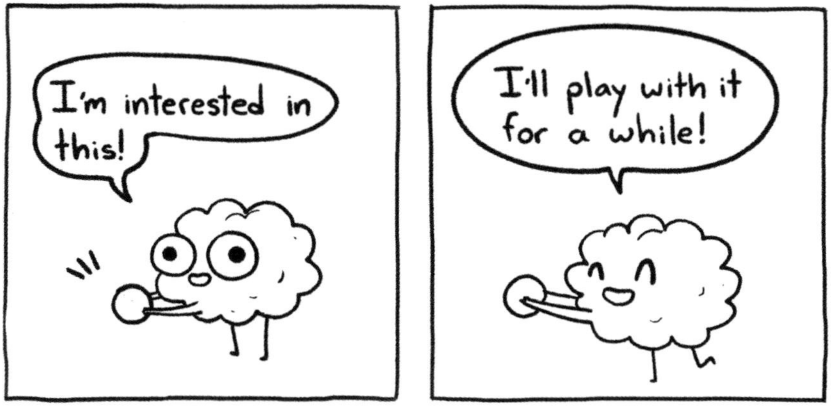
I'm interested in this!
I'll play with it for a while!

HYPERFIXATING

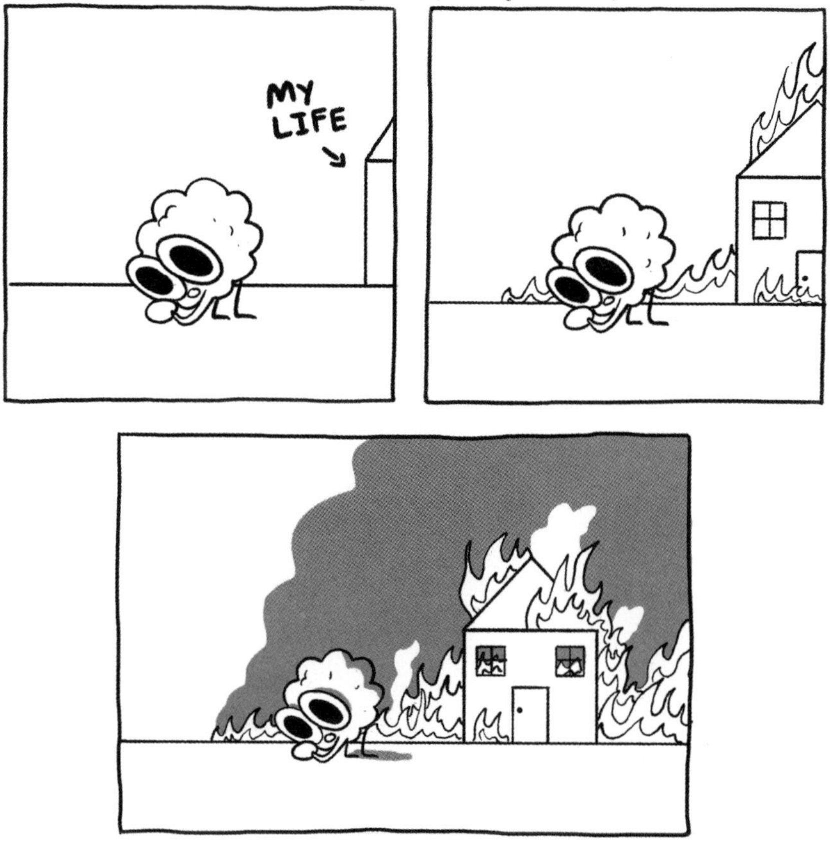
MY LIFE

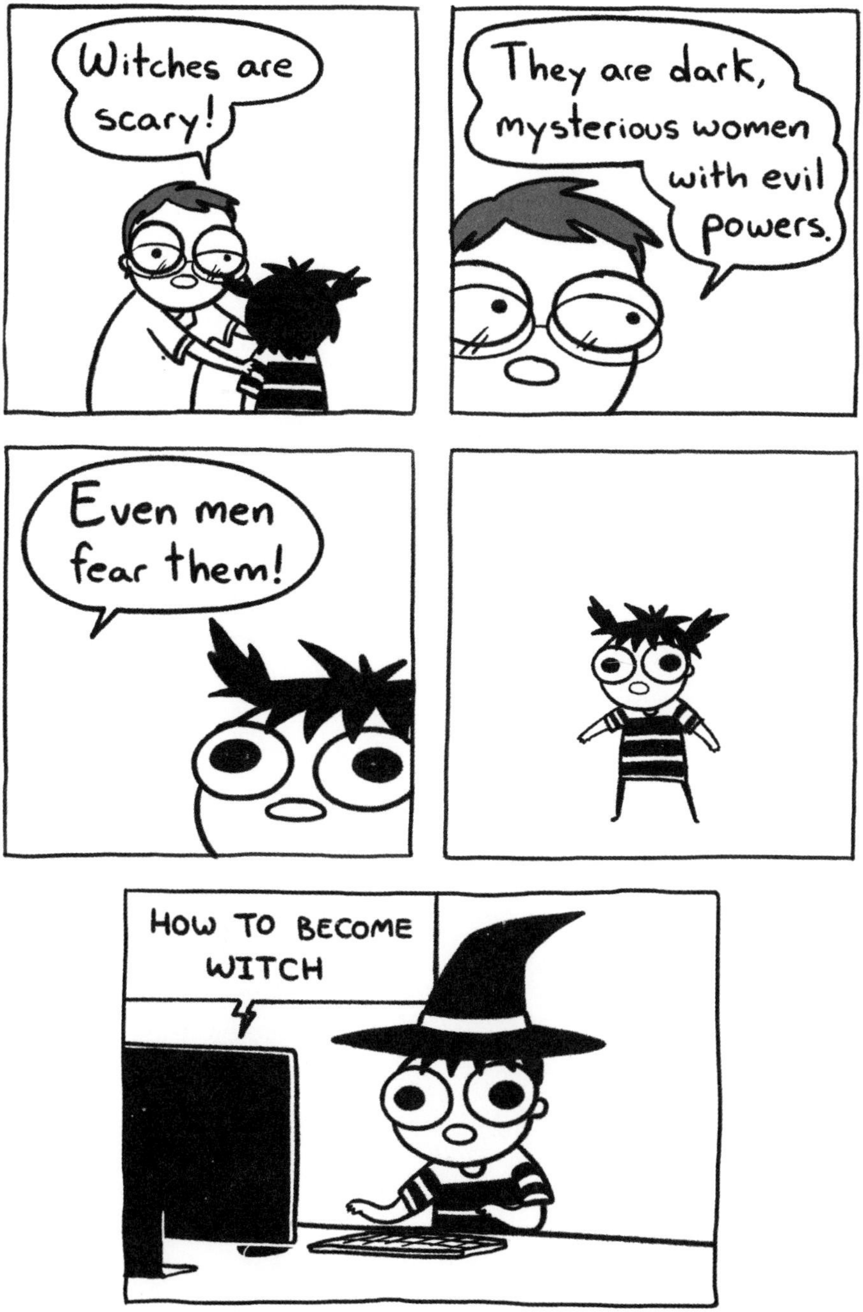
Witches are scary!
They are dark, mysterious women with evil powers.
Even men fear them!
HOW TO BECOME WITCH

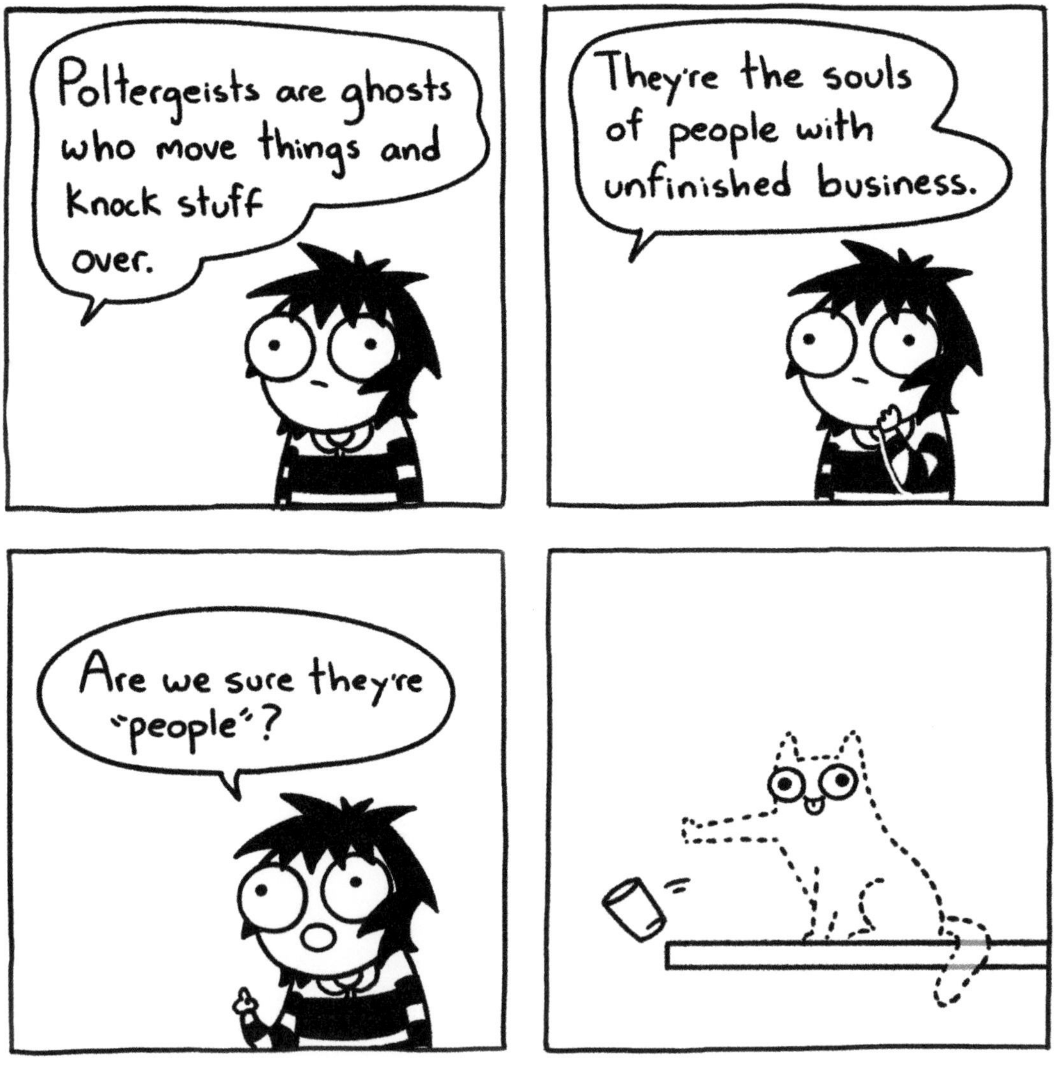
Poltergeists are ghosts who move things and knock stuff over.
They're the souls of people with unfinished business.
Are we sure they're "people"?

But who will adopt this BLIND cat?
LATER:

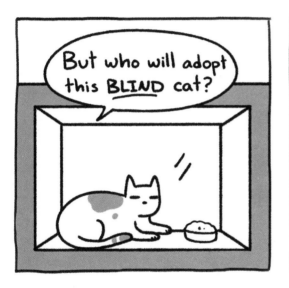

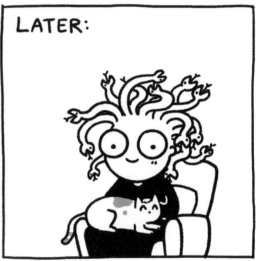

MY STYLE

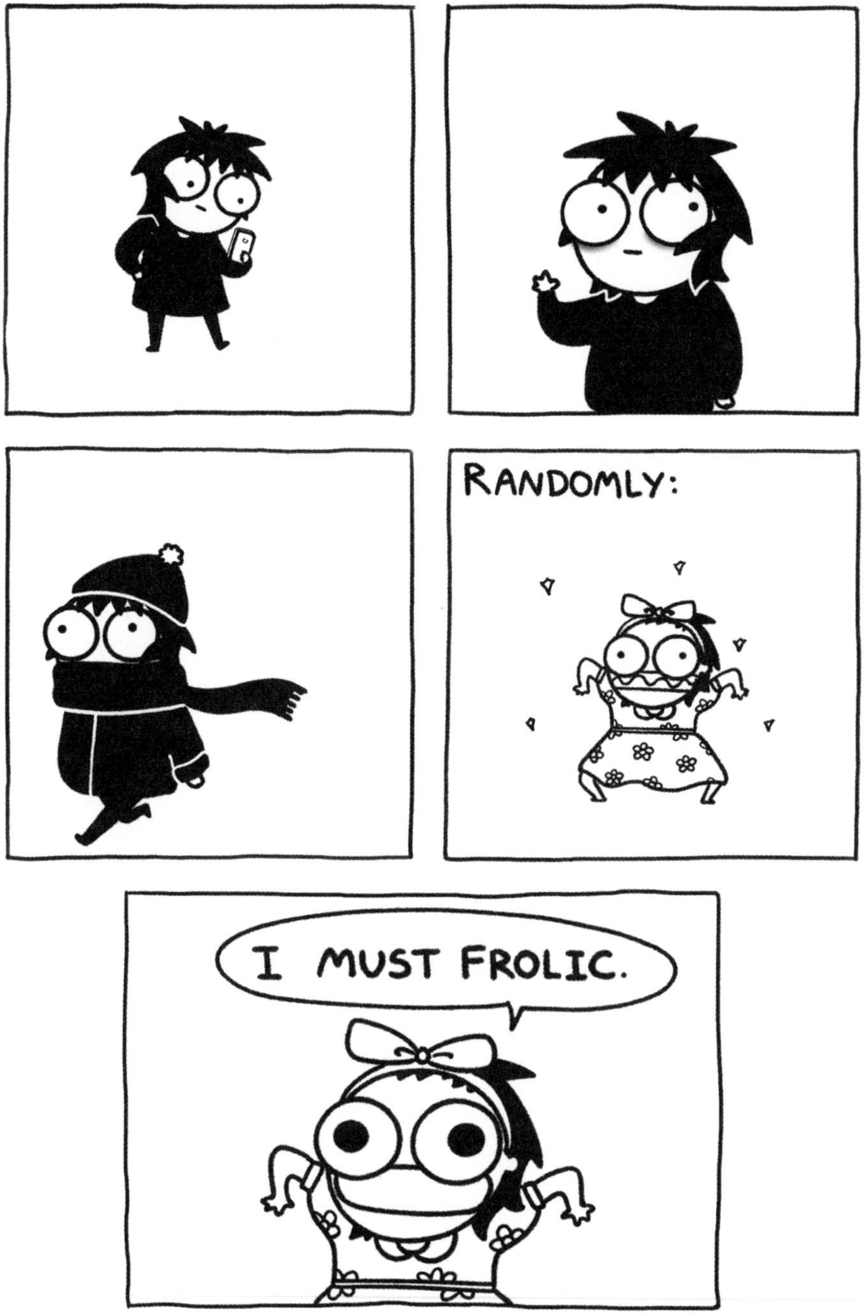
RANDOMLY:
I MUST FROLIC.

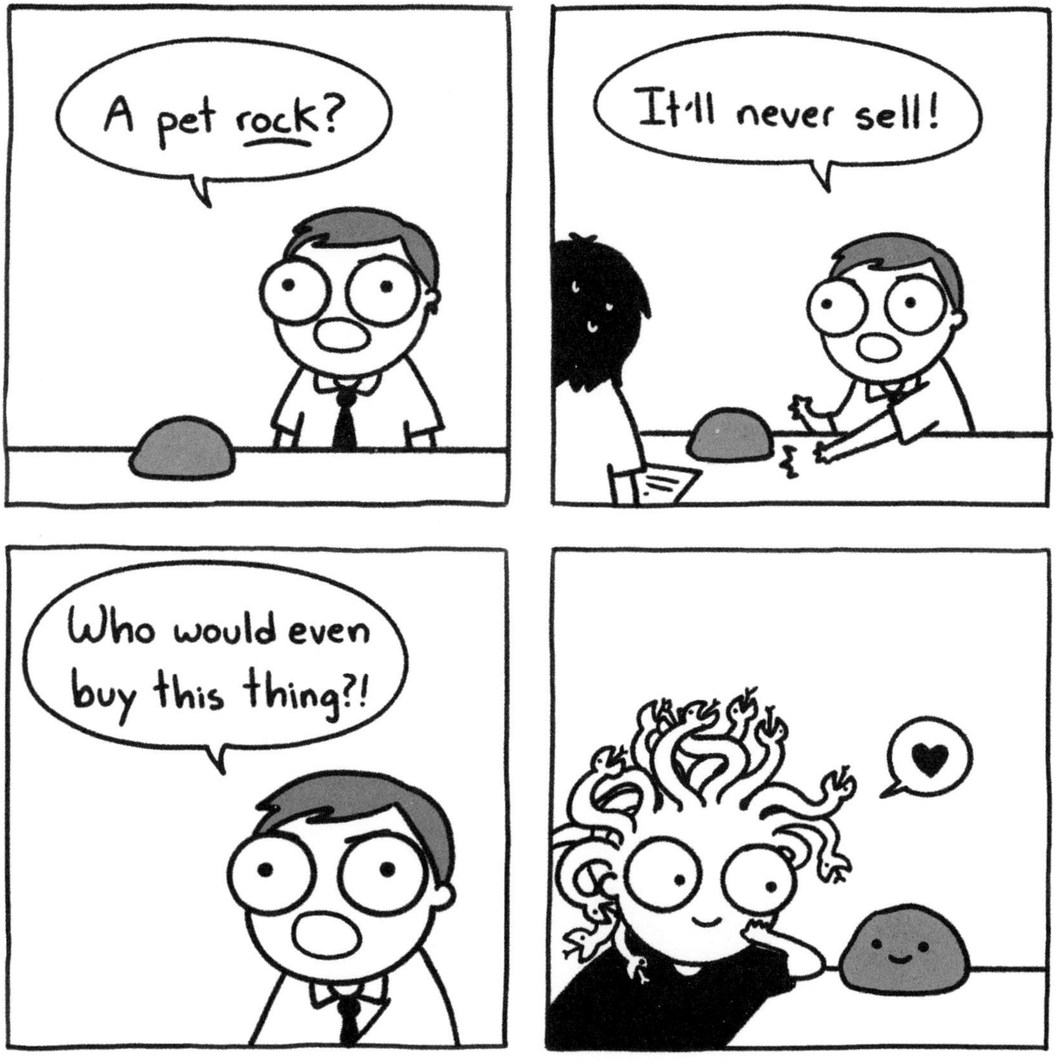
A pet rock?
It'll never sell!
Who would even buy this thing?!

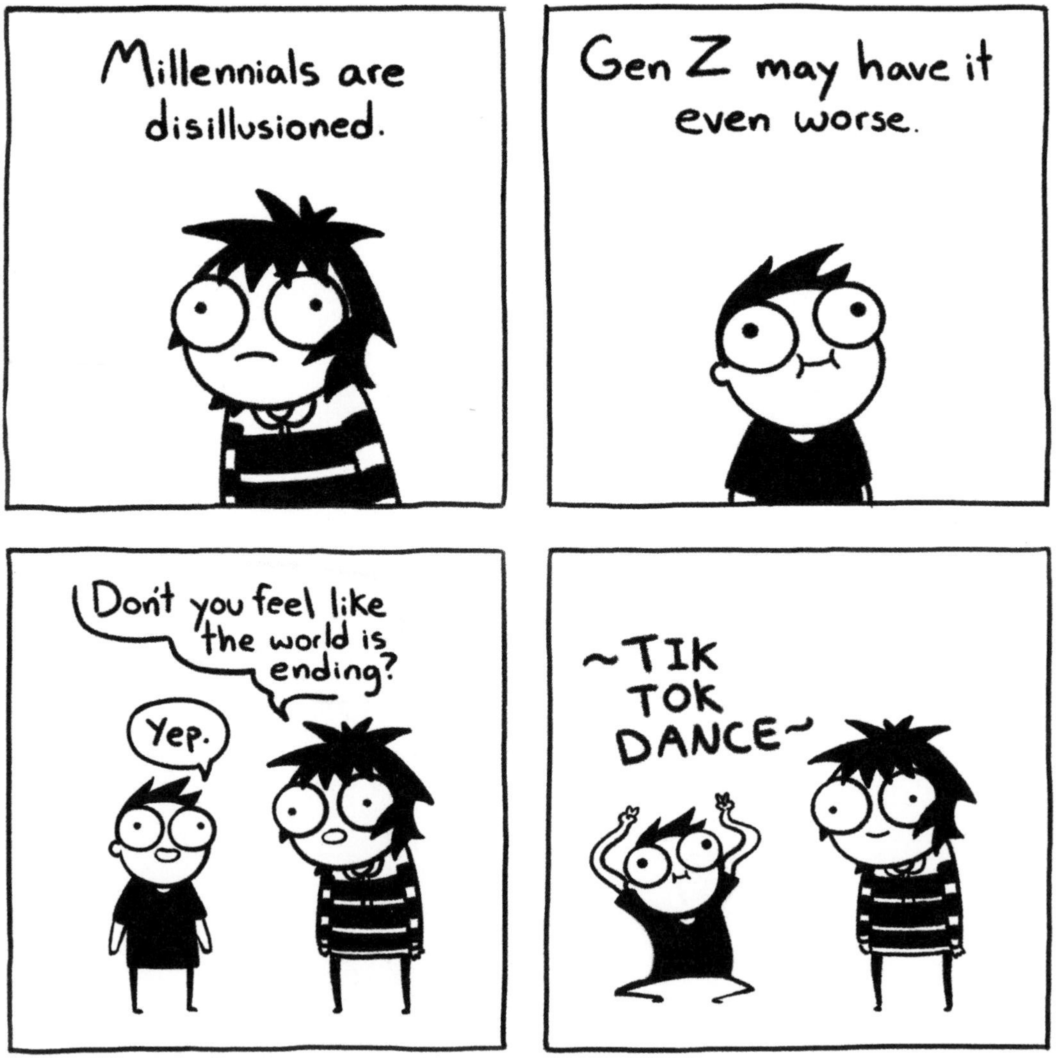
Millennials are disillusioned.
Gen Z may have it even worse.
Don't you feel like the world is ending?
Yep.
~TIK TOK DANCE~

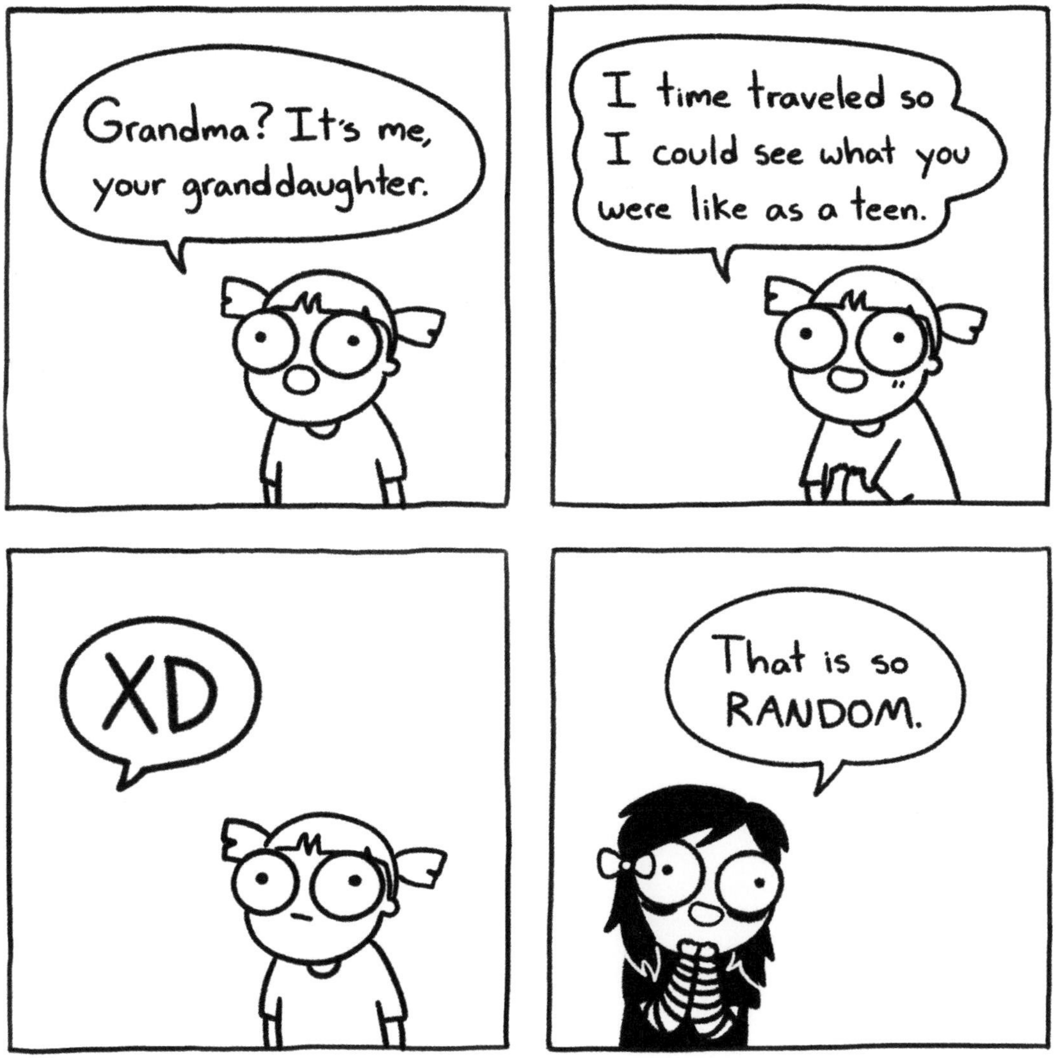
Grandma? It's me, your granddaughter.
I time traveled so I could see what you were like as a teen.
XD
That is so RANDOM.

HOW I TELL STORIES

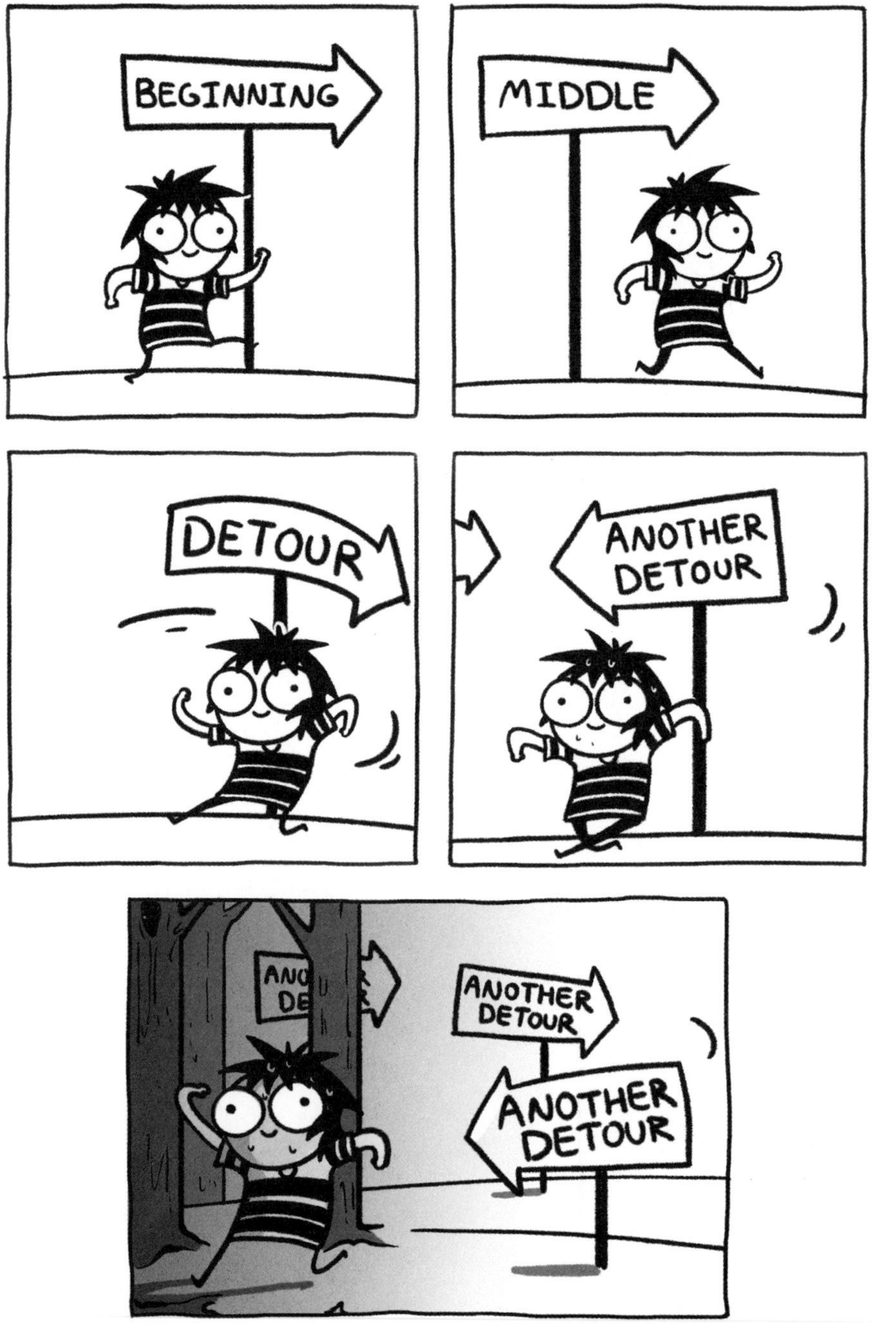
BEGINNING
MIDDLE
DETOUR
ANOTHER DETOUR
ANOTHER DETOUR
ANOTHER DETOUR

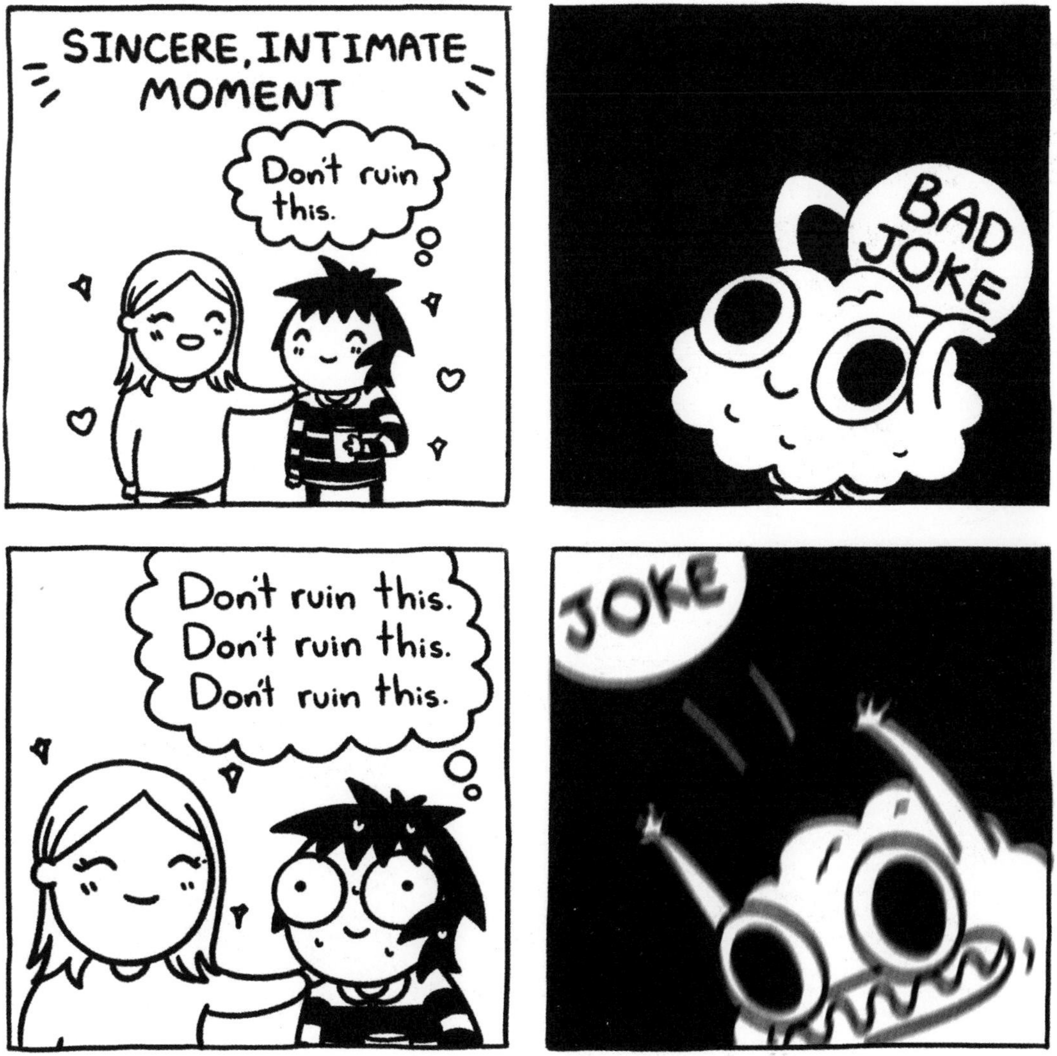
SINCERE, INTIMATE MOMENT
Don't ruin this.
BAD JOKE
Don't ruin this.
Don't ruin this.
Don't ruin this.
JOKE

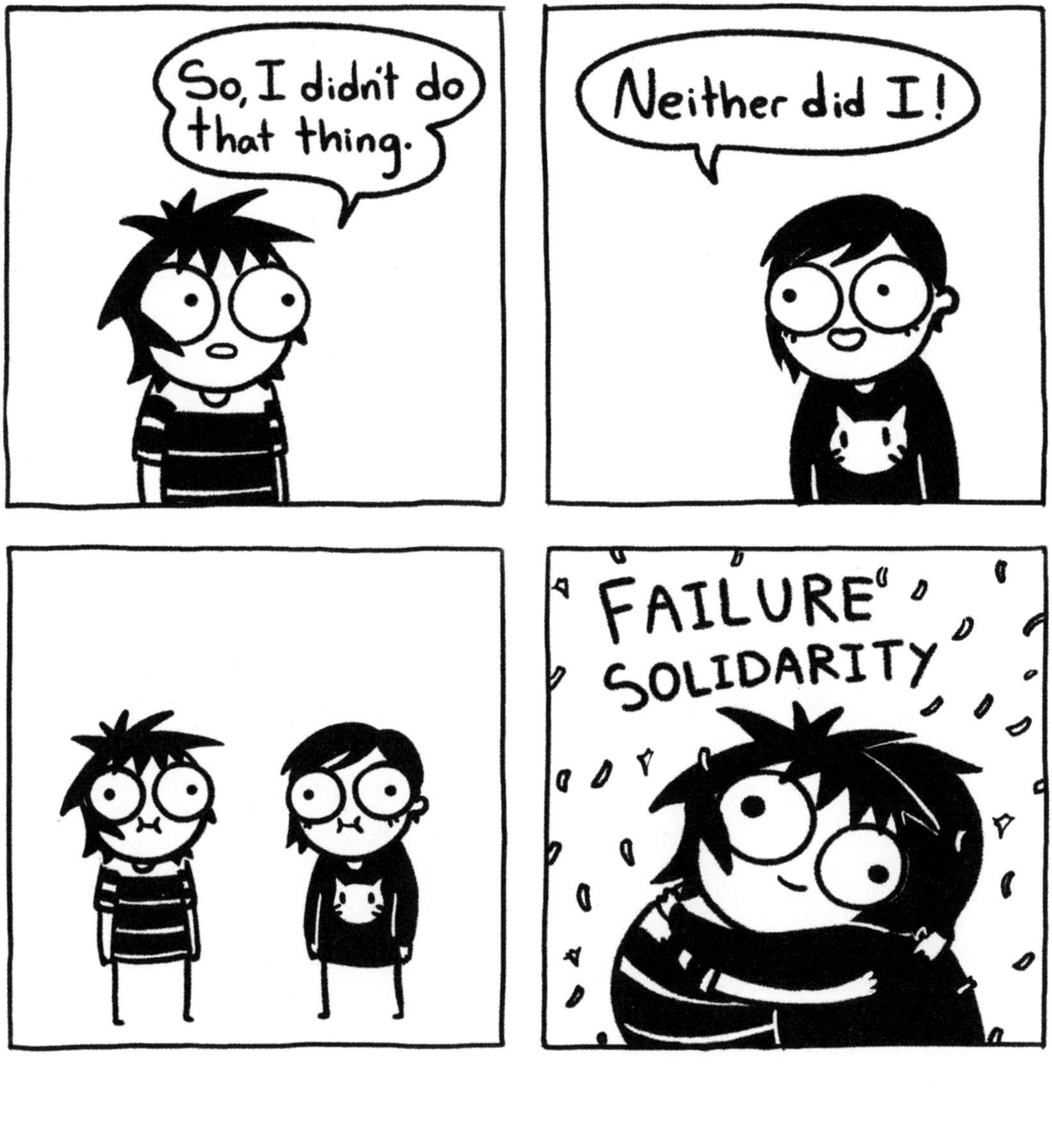
So, I didn't do that thing.
Neither did I!
FAILURE SOLIDARITY

QUARANTINE BRAIN

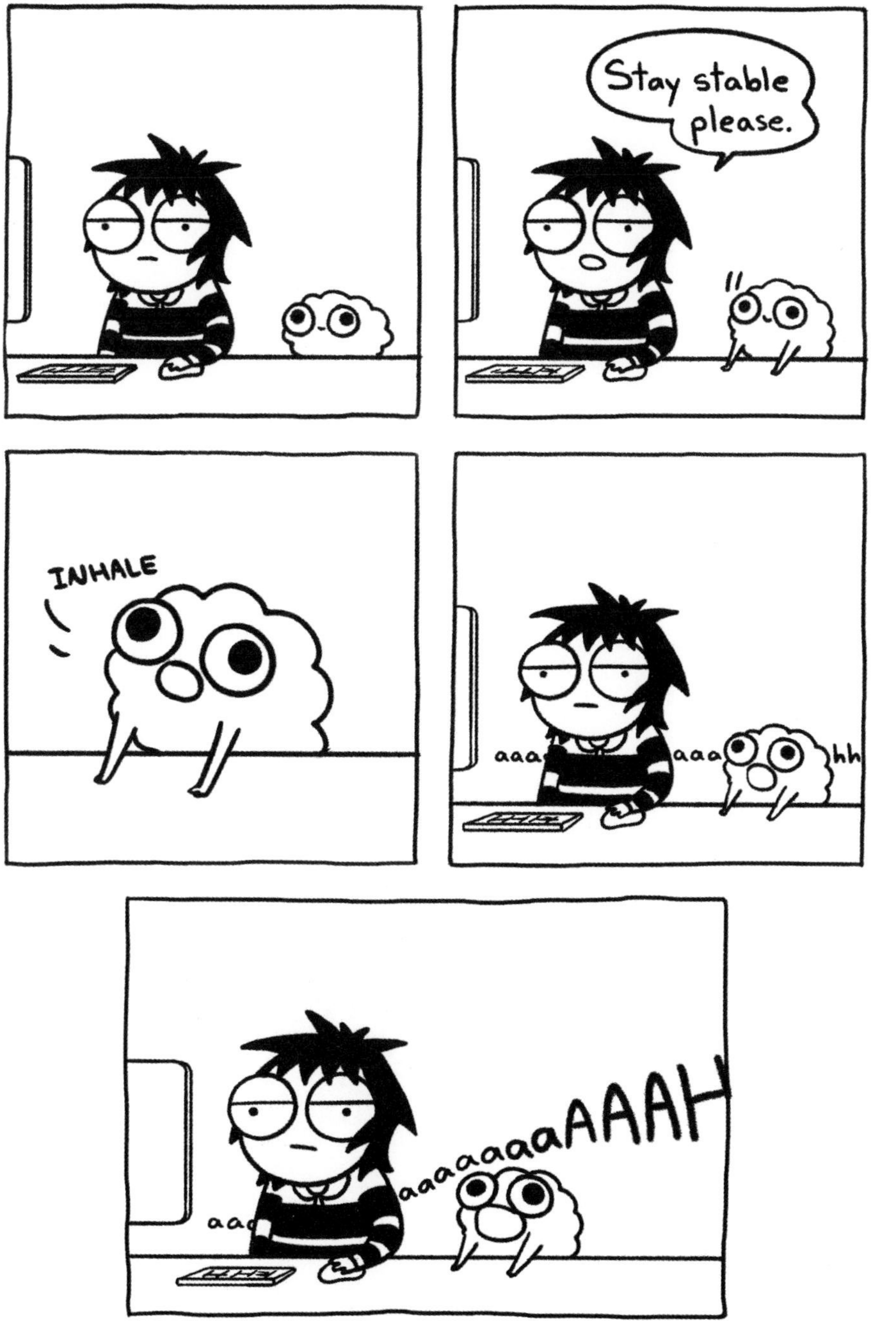
Stay stable please.
INHALE
aaa
aaa
hh
aa
aaaaaaaaAAAH

DRACULA'S CAT

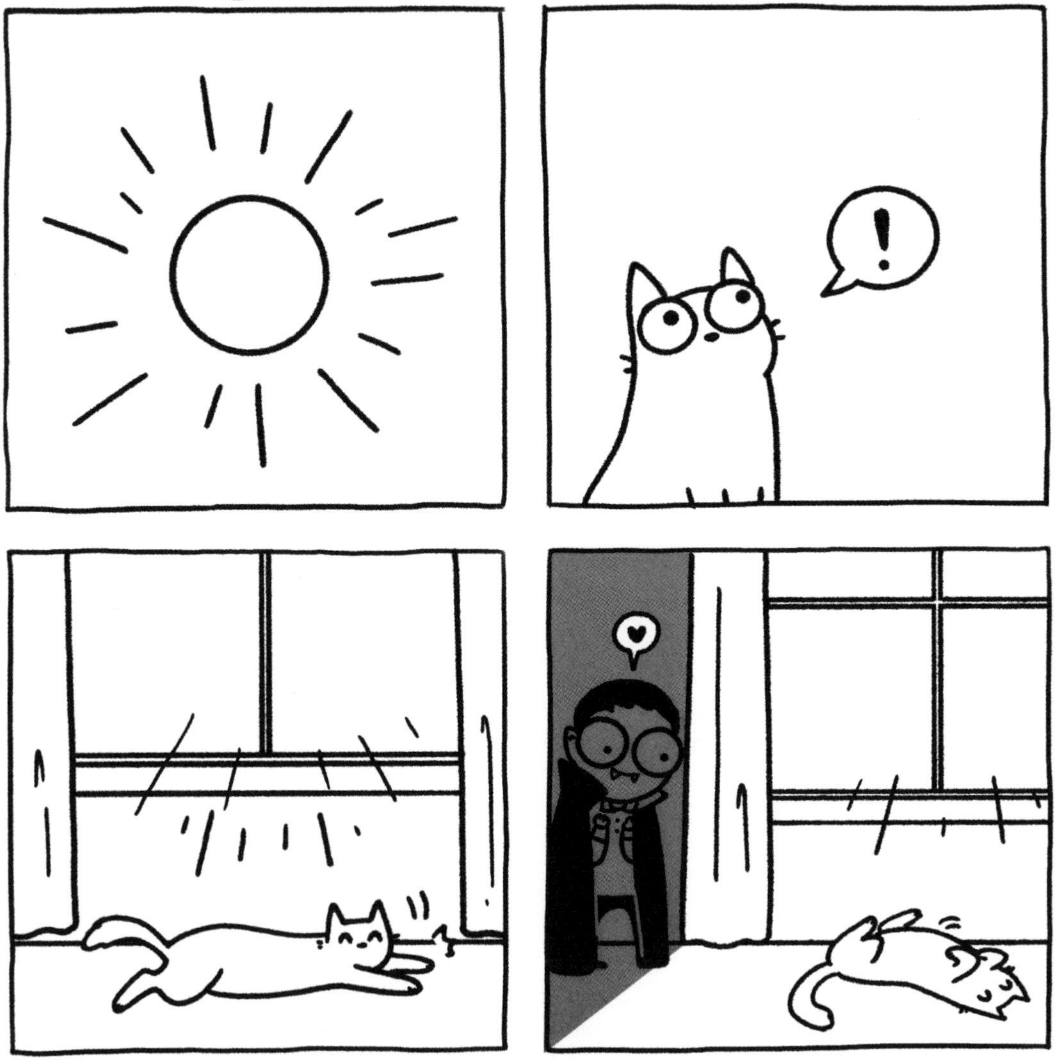
!

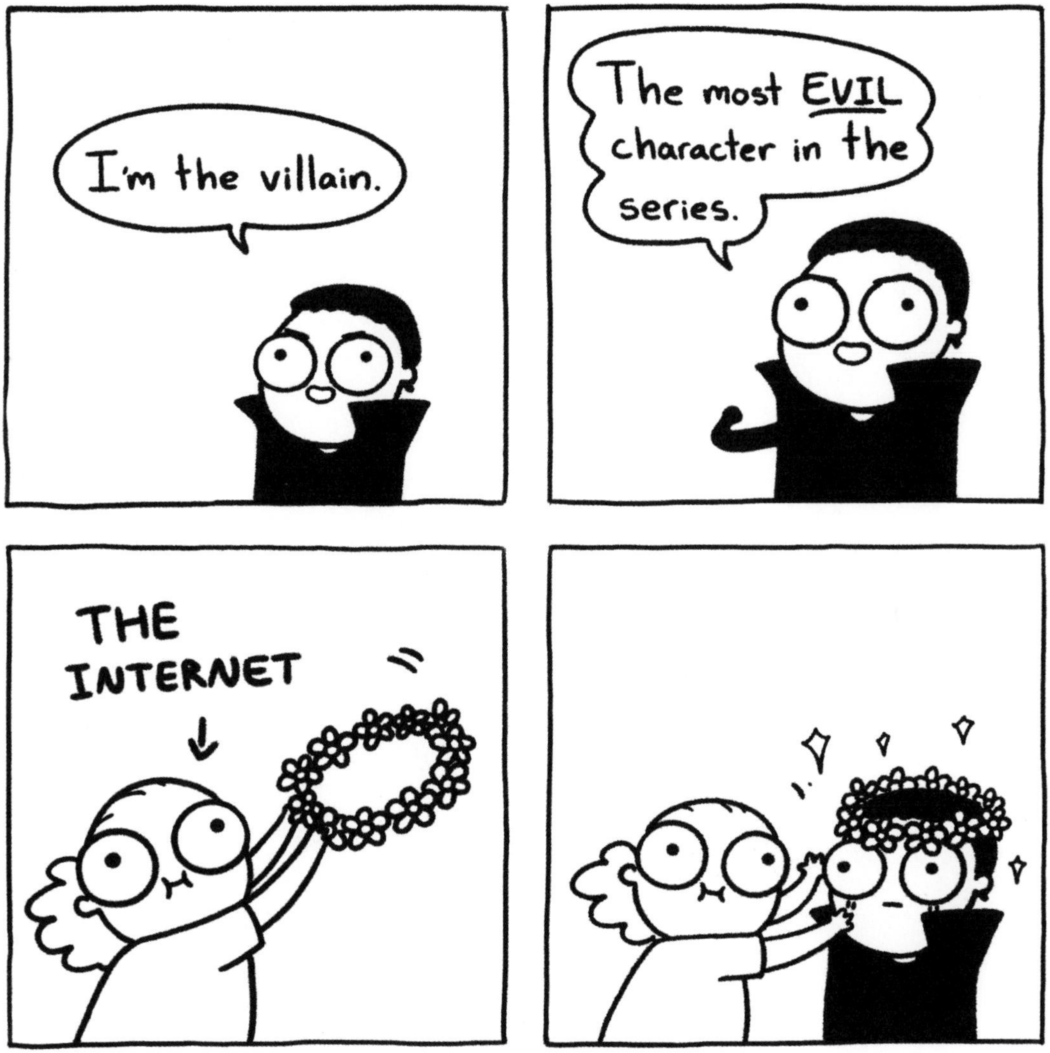
I'm the villain.
The most EVIL character in the series.
THE INTERNET

DEATH TRAPS

CLAMP
CLAMP

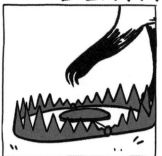

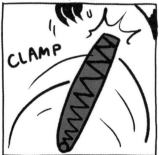

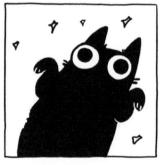

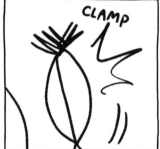

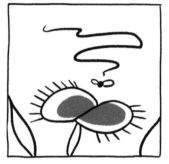

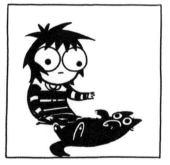

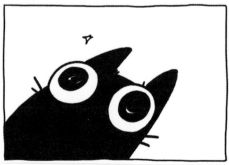

FIGHT!

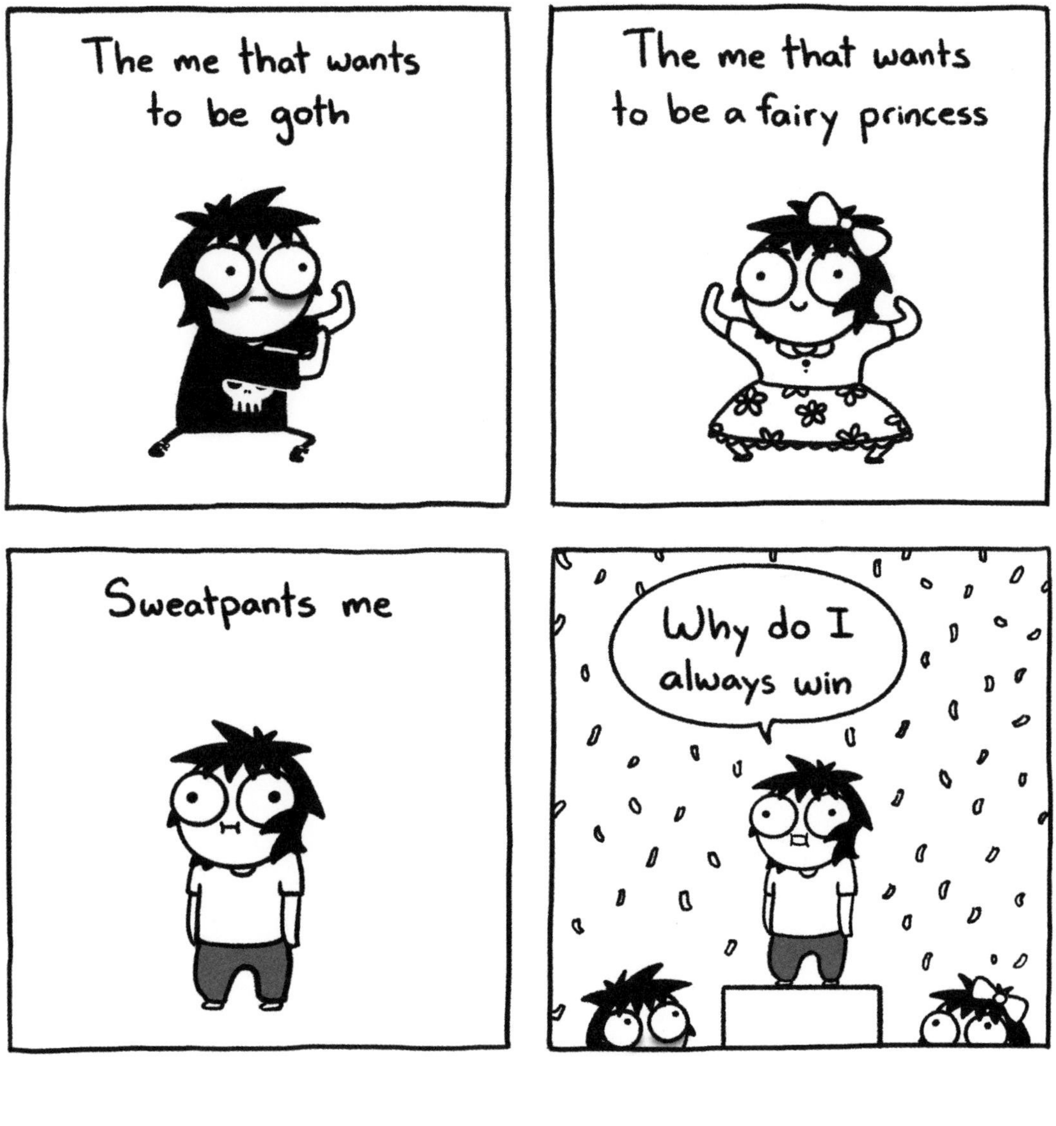

The me that wants to be goth
The me that wants to be a fairy princess
Sweatpants me
Why do I always win

Always trying to be better than everyone

Always trying to be smarter

Always trying to be superior

Just being kind

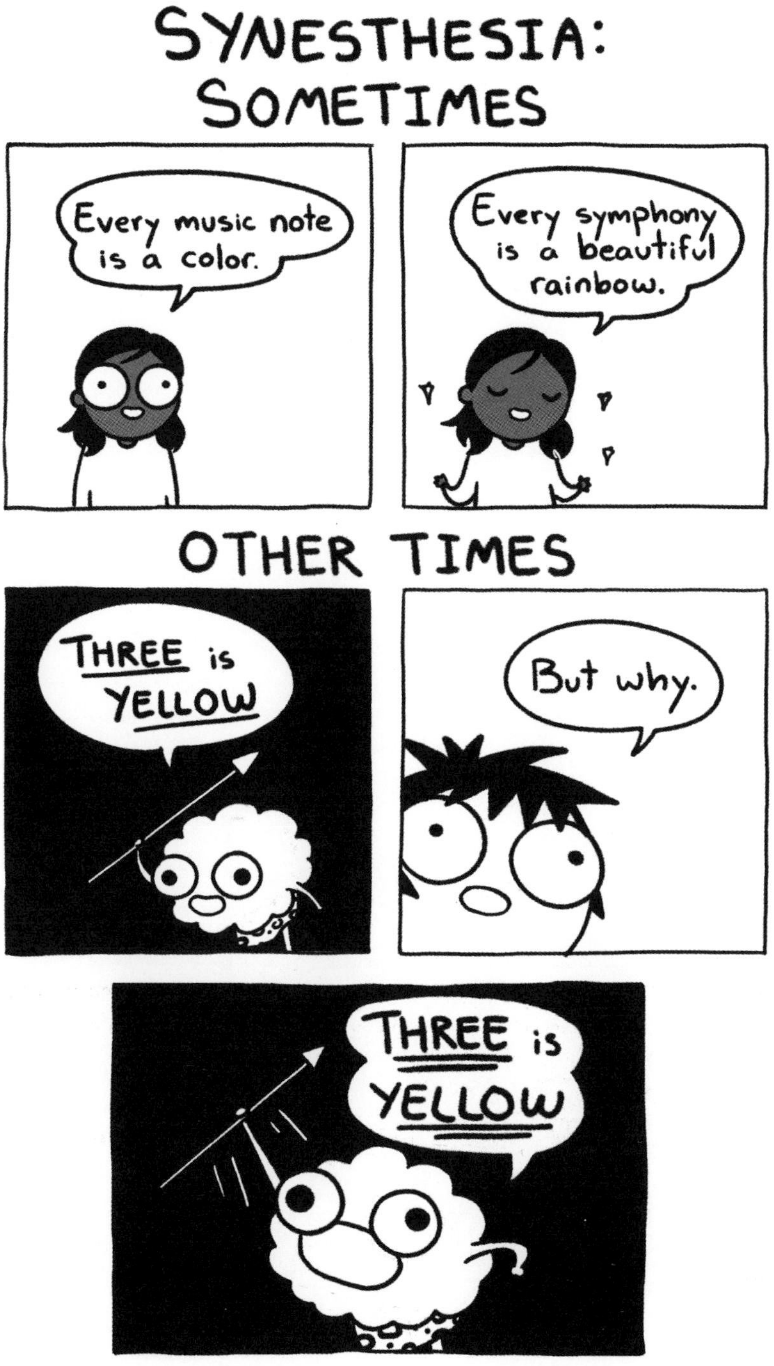
SYNESTHESIA:
SOMETIMES
Every music note is a color.
Every symphony is a beautiful rainbow.
OTHER TIMES
THREE is YELLOW
But why.
THREE is YELLOW

Common Women's Interests

ANIMALS
MAKEUP
FASHION
TRUE CRIME
And that's how they dissolved the body!
CLAP
CLAP
CLAP

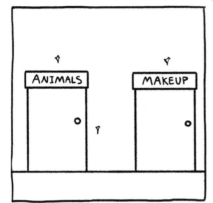

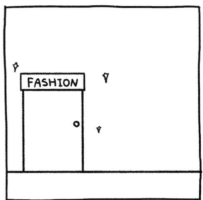

SUDDENLY FINDING A NEW OBSESSION

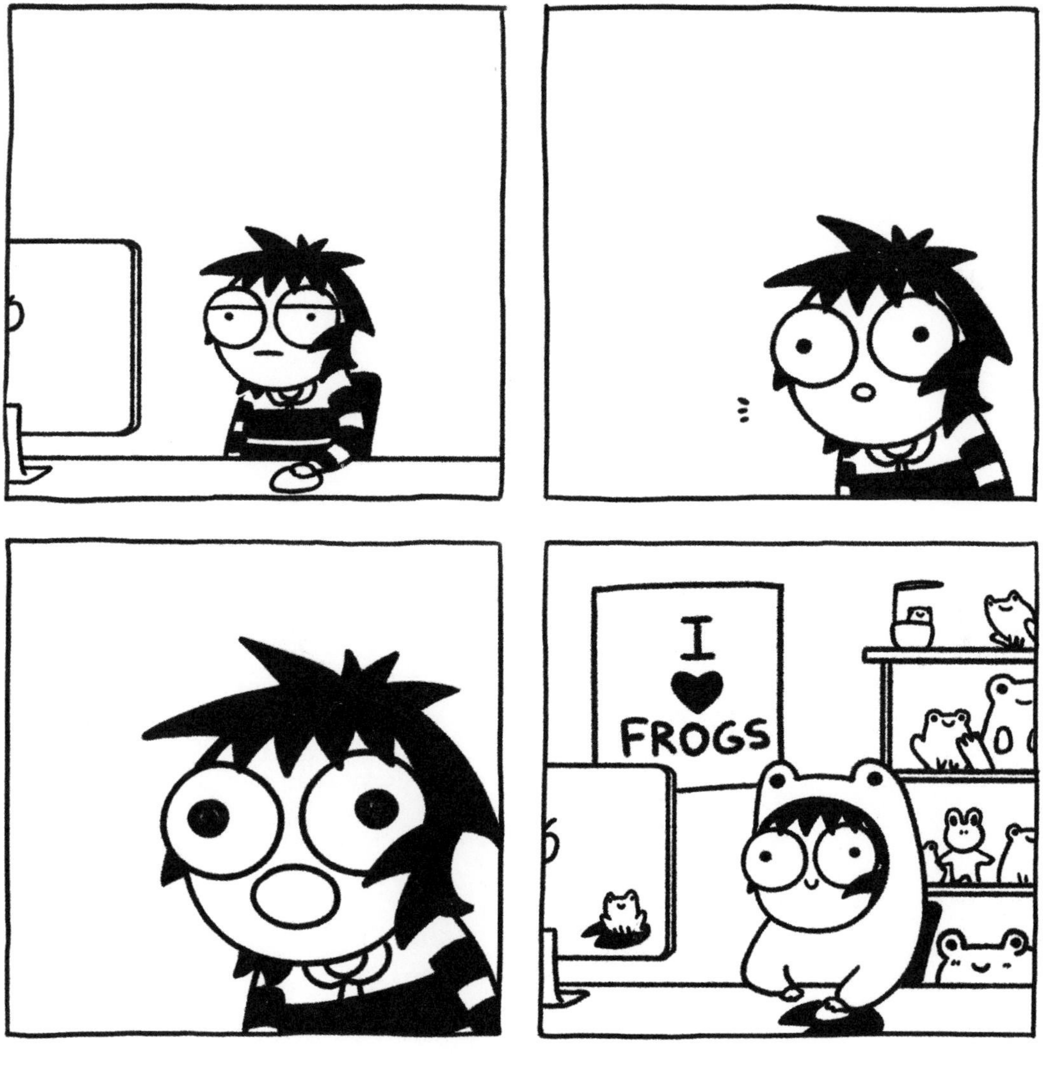
I
FROGS

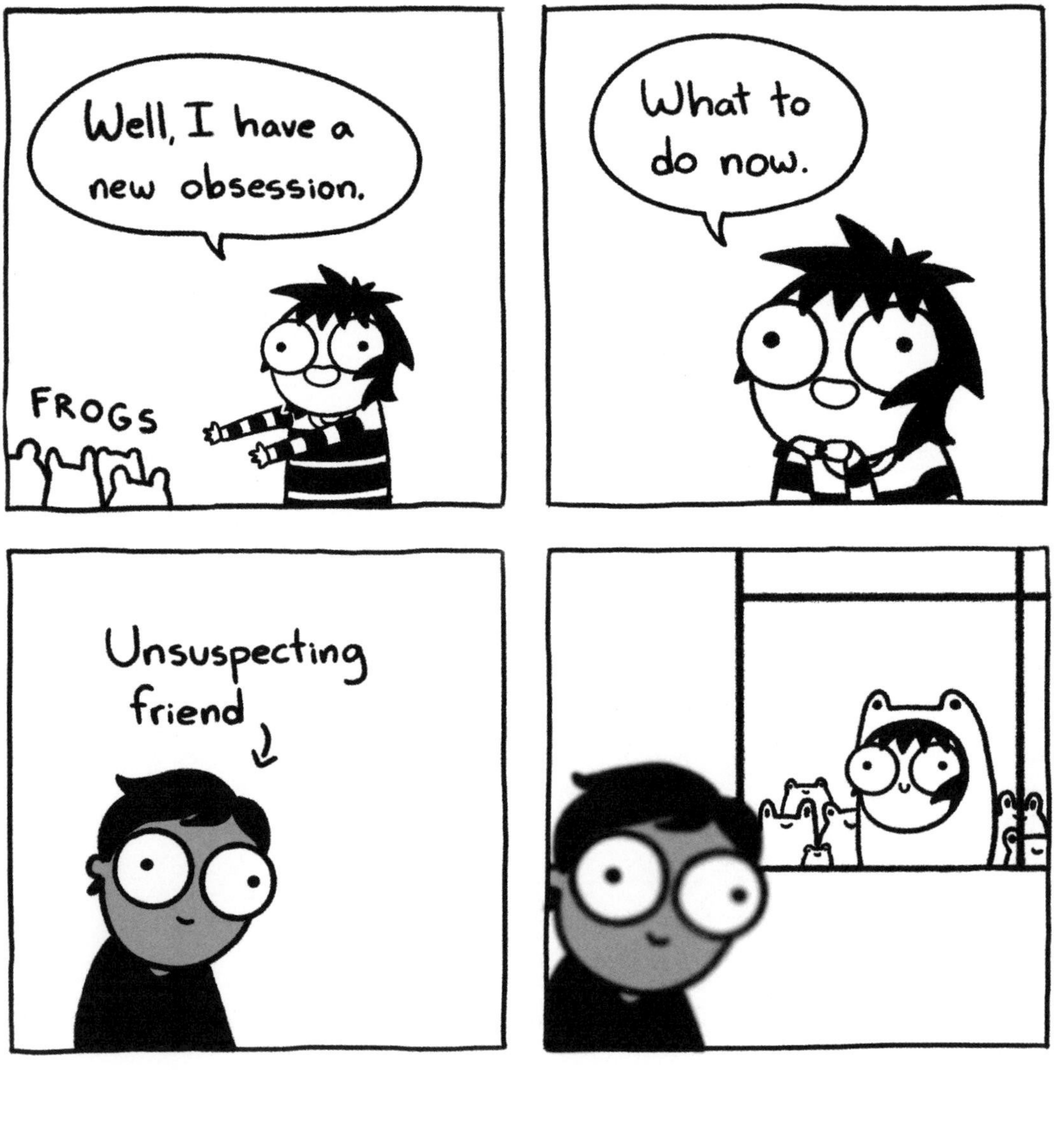
Well, I have a new obsession.
FROGS
What to do now.
Unsuspecting friend

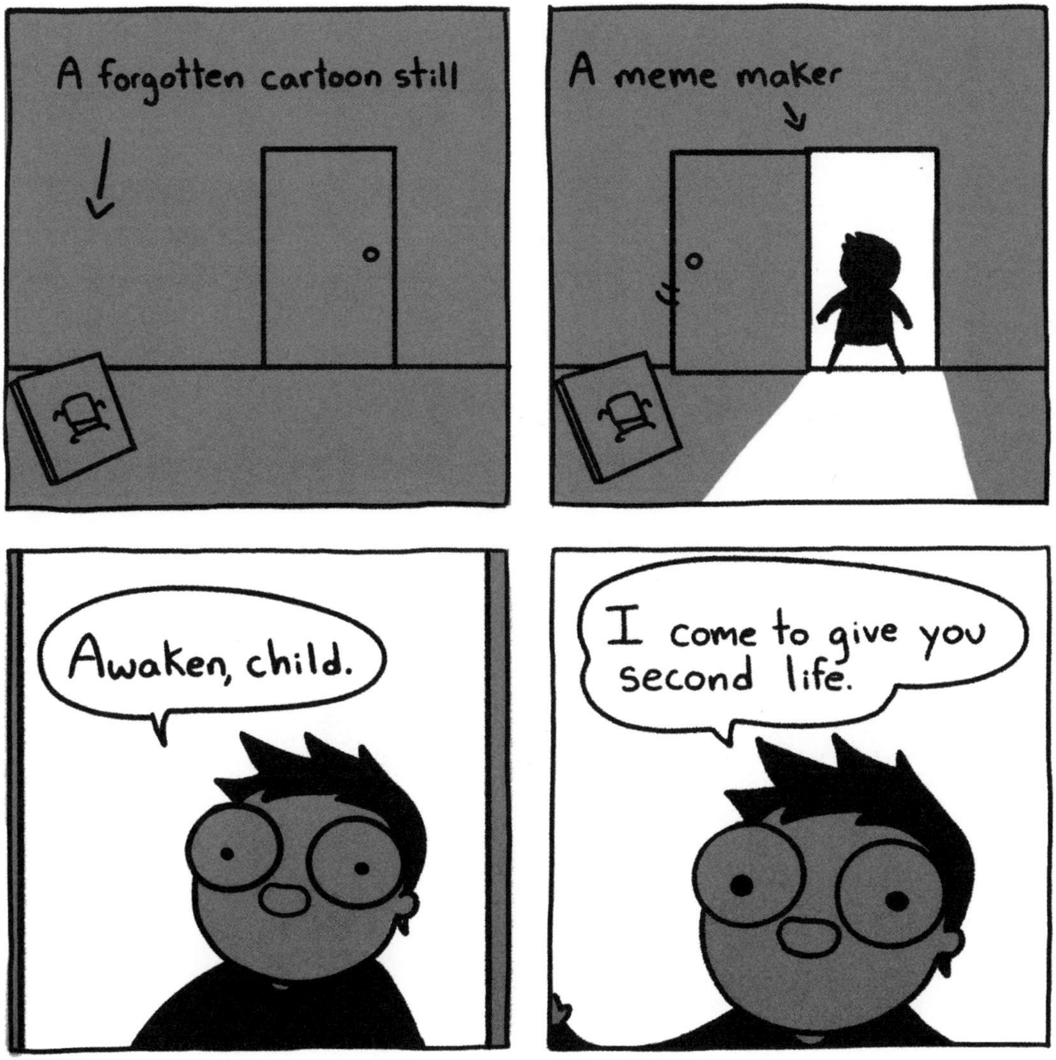
A forgotten cartoon still
A meme maker
Awaken, child.
I come to give you second life.

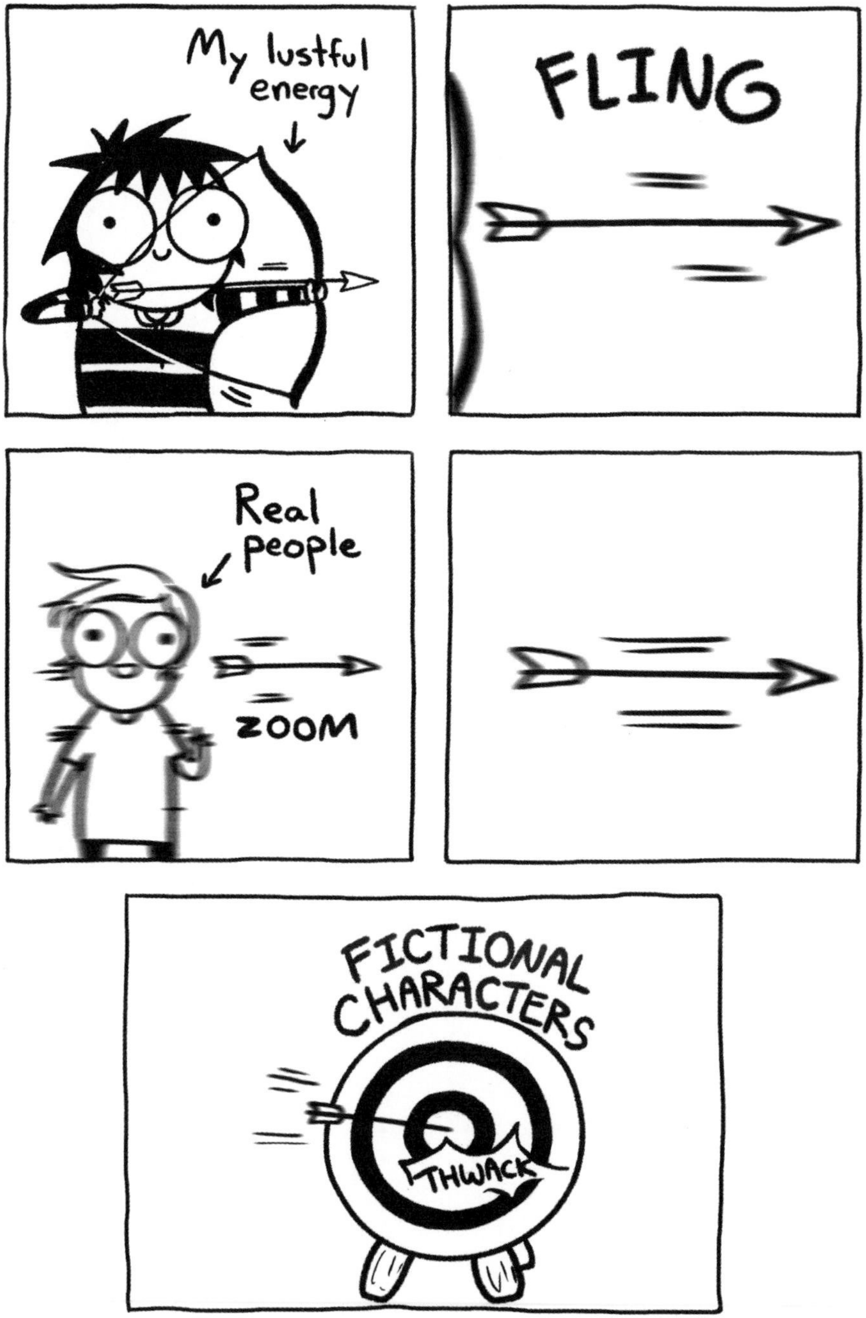
My lustful energy
FLING
Real people
ZOOM
FICTIONAL CHARACTERS
THWACK

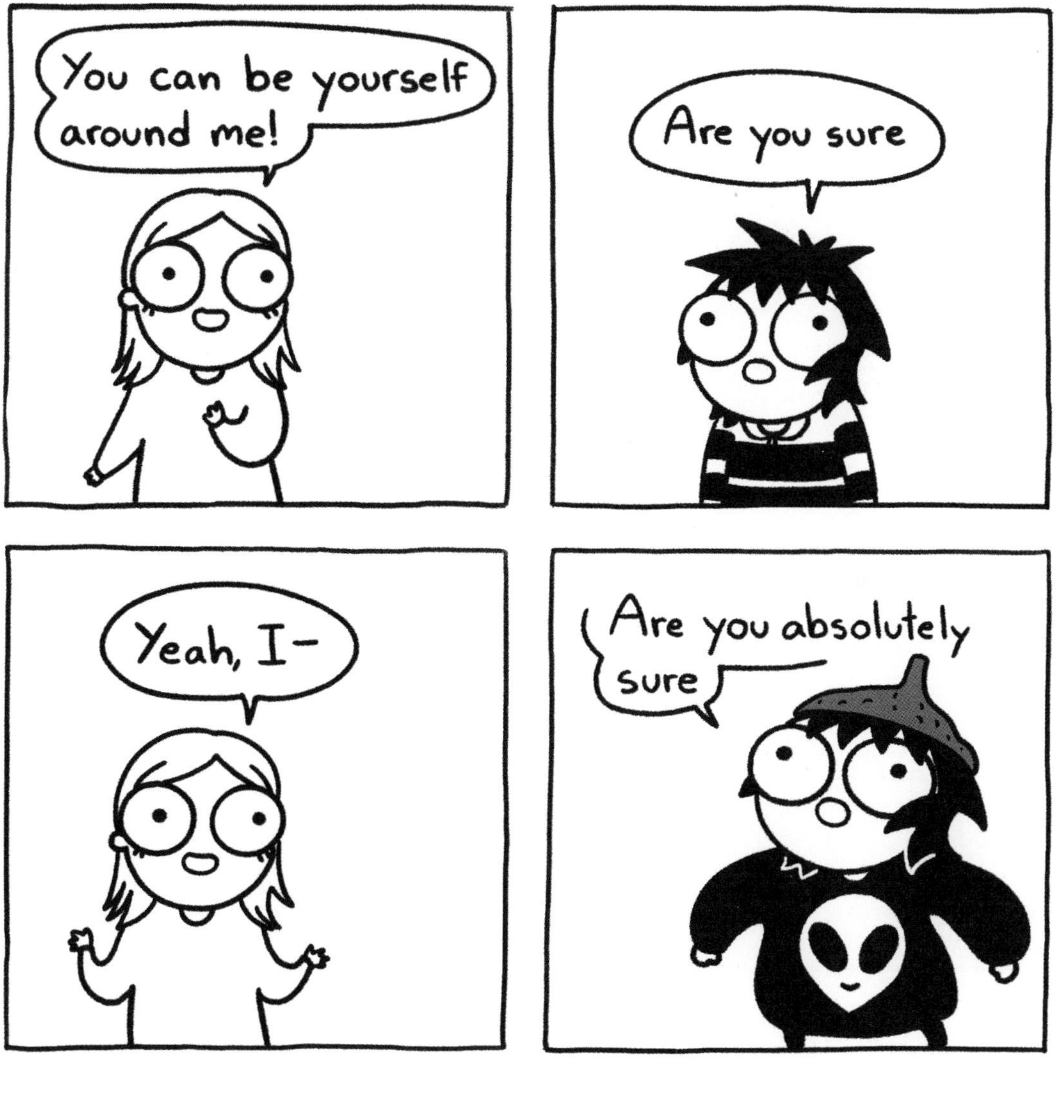
You can be yourself around me!
Are you sure
Yeah, I-
Are you absolutely sure

Staying up late is FUN!!!
THUD
The Sadness is coming.

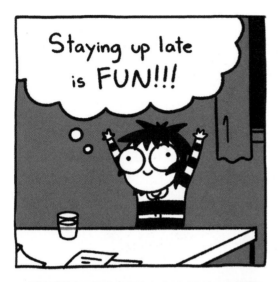

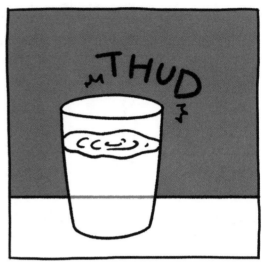

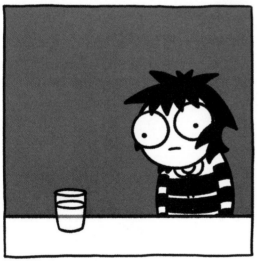

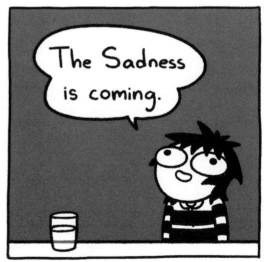

CRYPTID CLUB

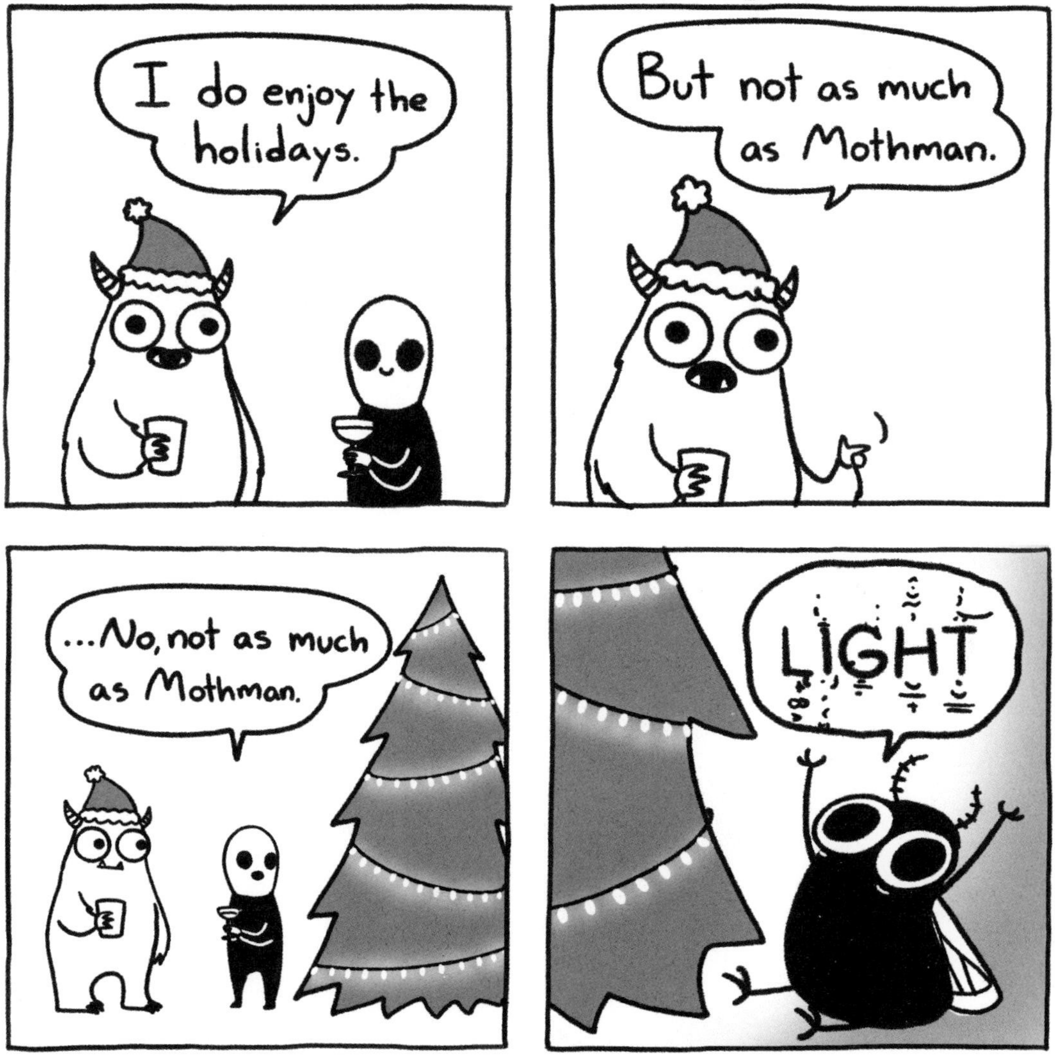
I do enjoy the holidays.
But not as much as Mothman.
...No, not as much as Mothman.
LIGHT

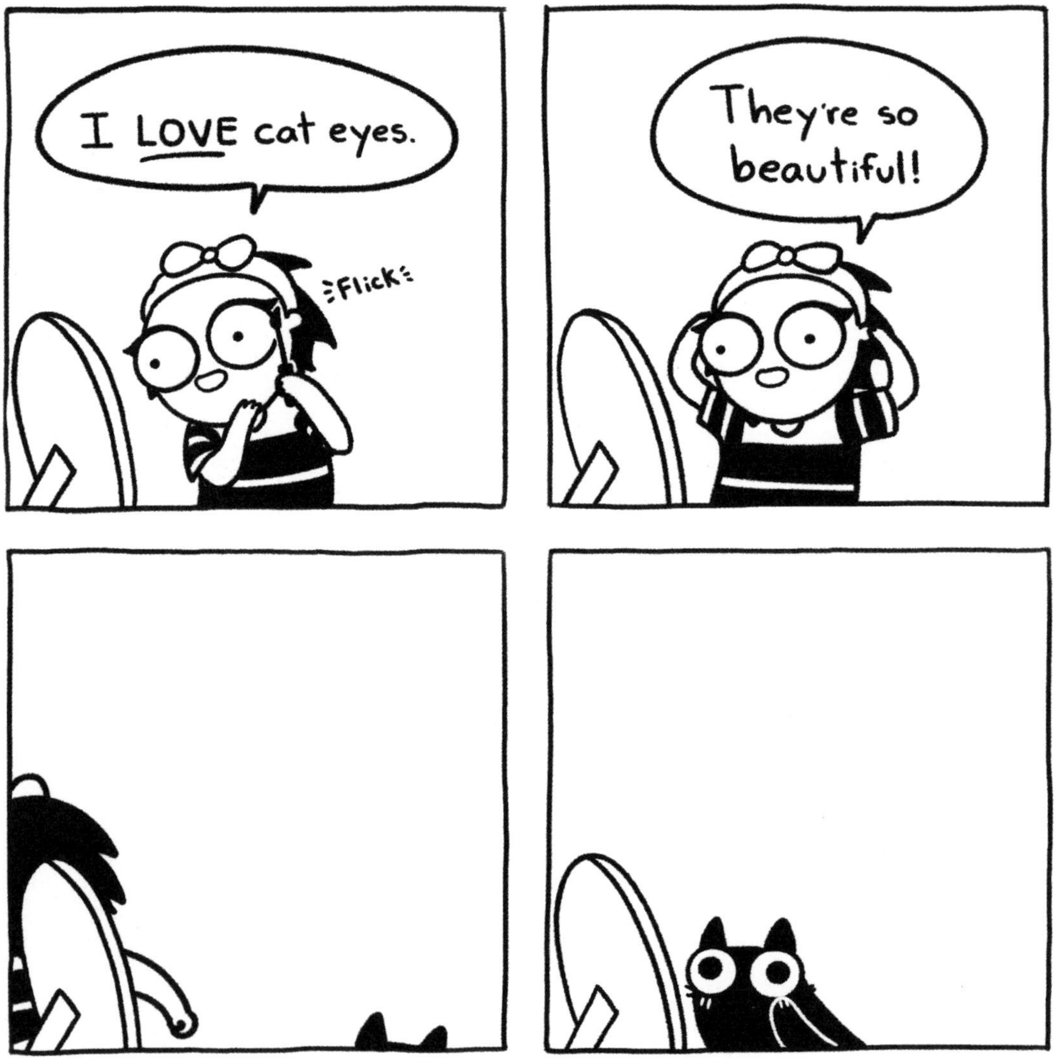
I LOVE cat eyes.
Flick
They're so beautiful!

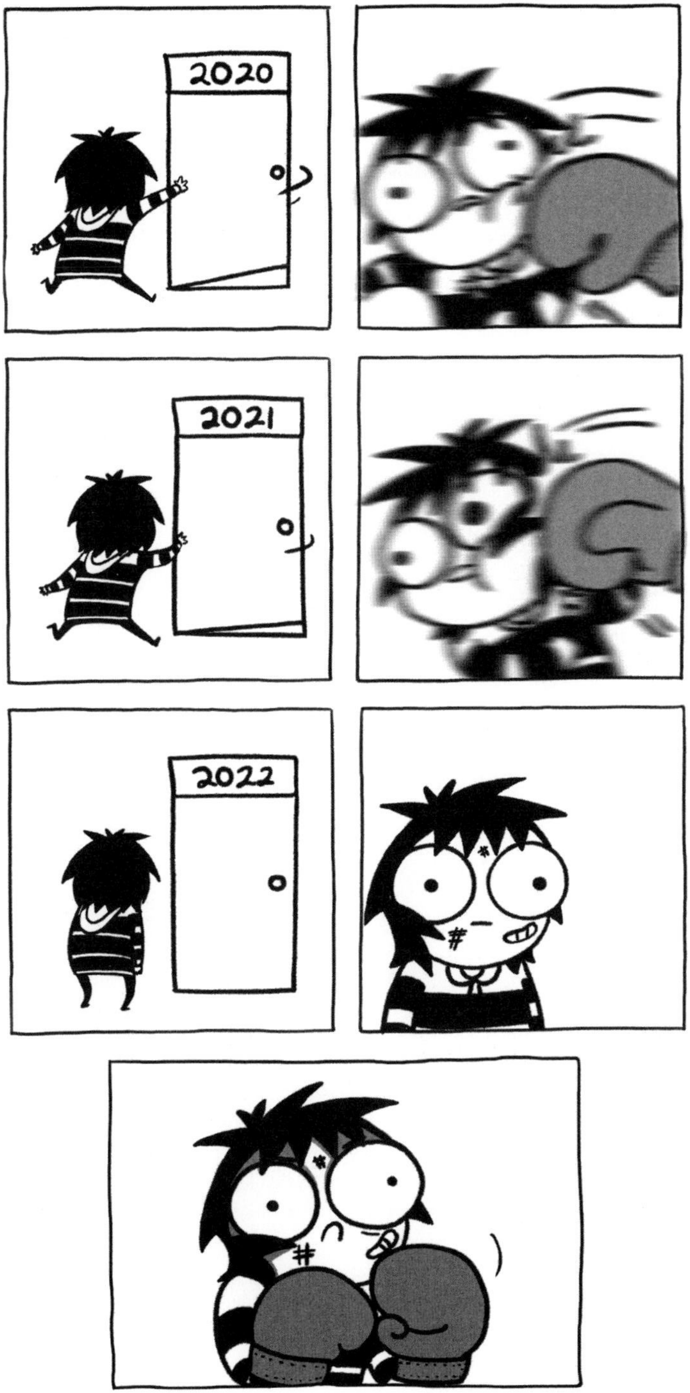
2020
2021
2022

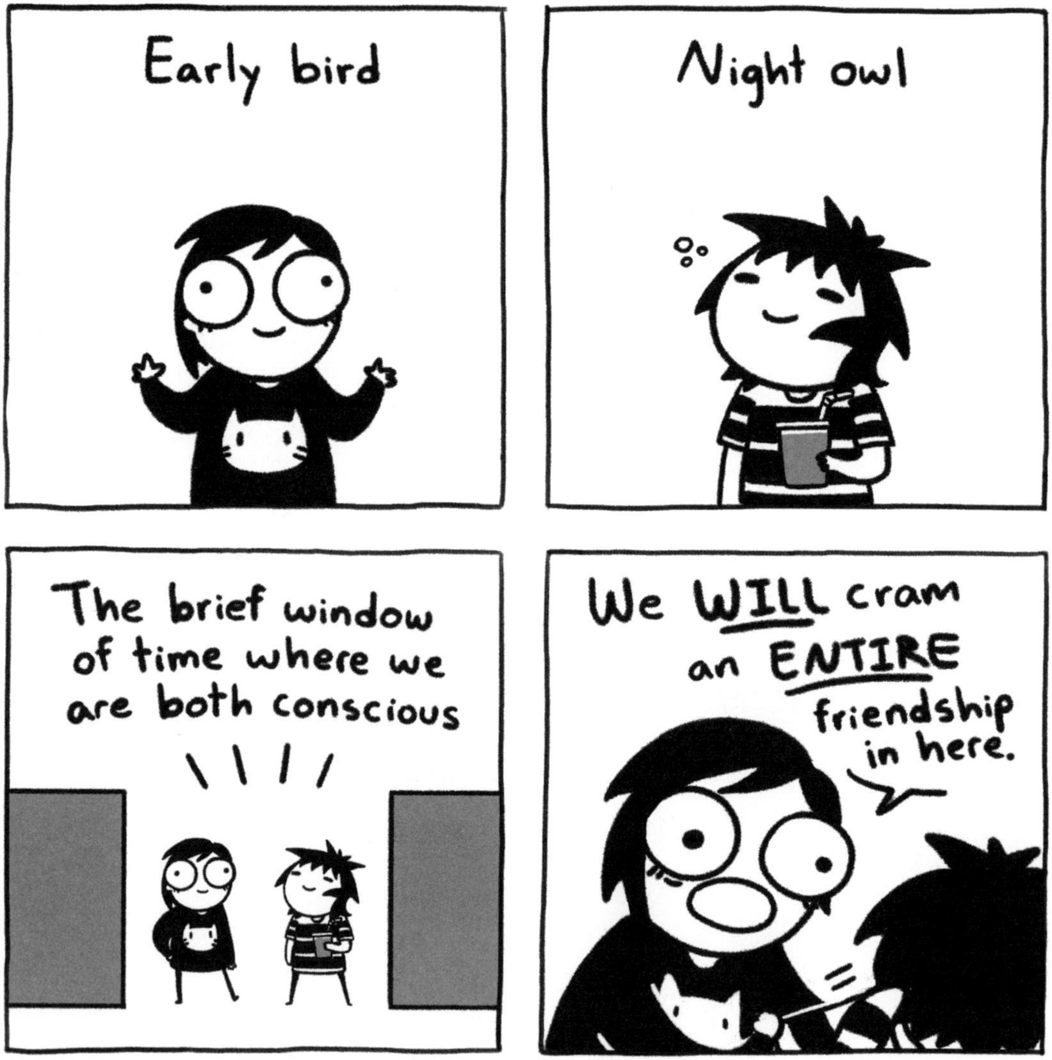
Early bird
Night owl
The brief window of time where we are both conscious
We WILL cram an ENTIRE friendship in here.

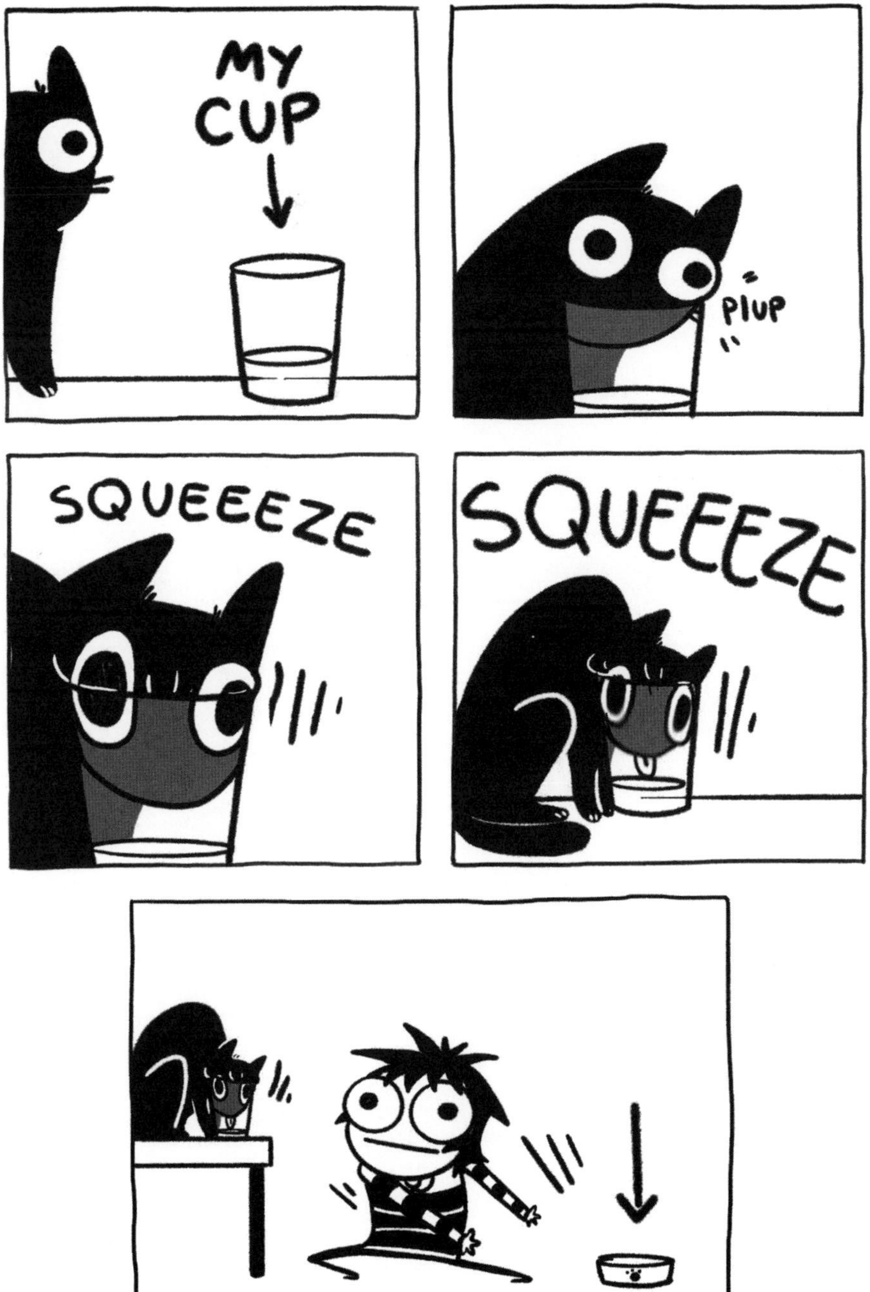
MY
CUP
PLUP
SQUEEEZE
SQUEEEZE

BROWSING THE INTERNET

SECRETS OF THE BERMUDATRIANGLE
How do I always end up here

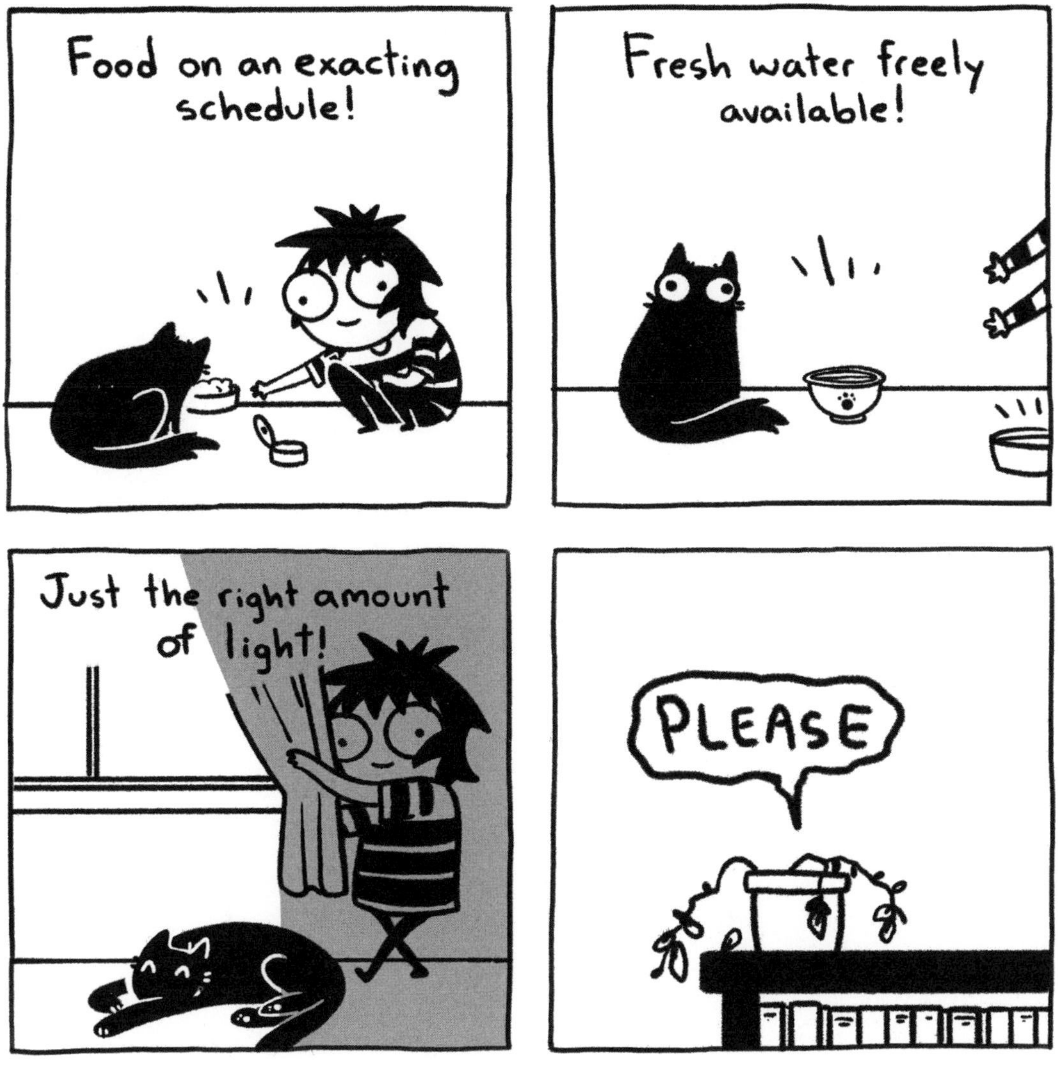
Food on an exacting schedule!
Fresh water freely available!
Just the right amount of light!
PLEASE

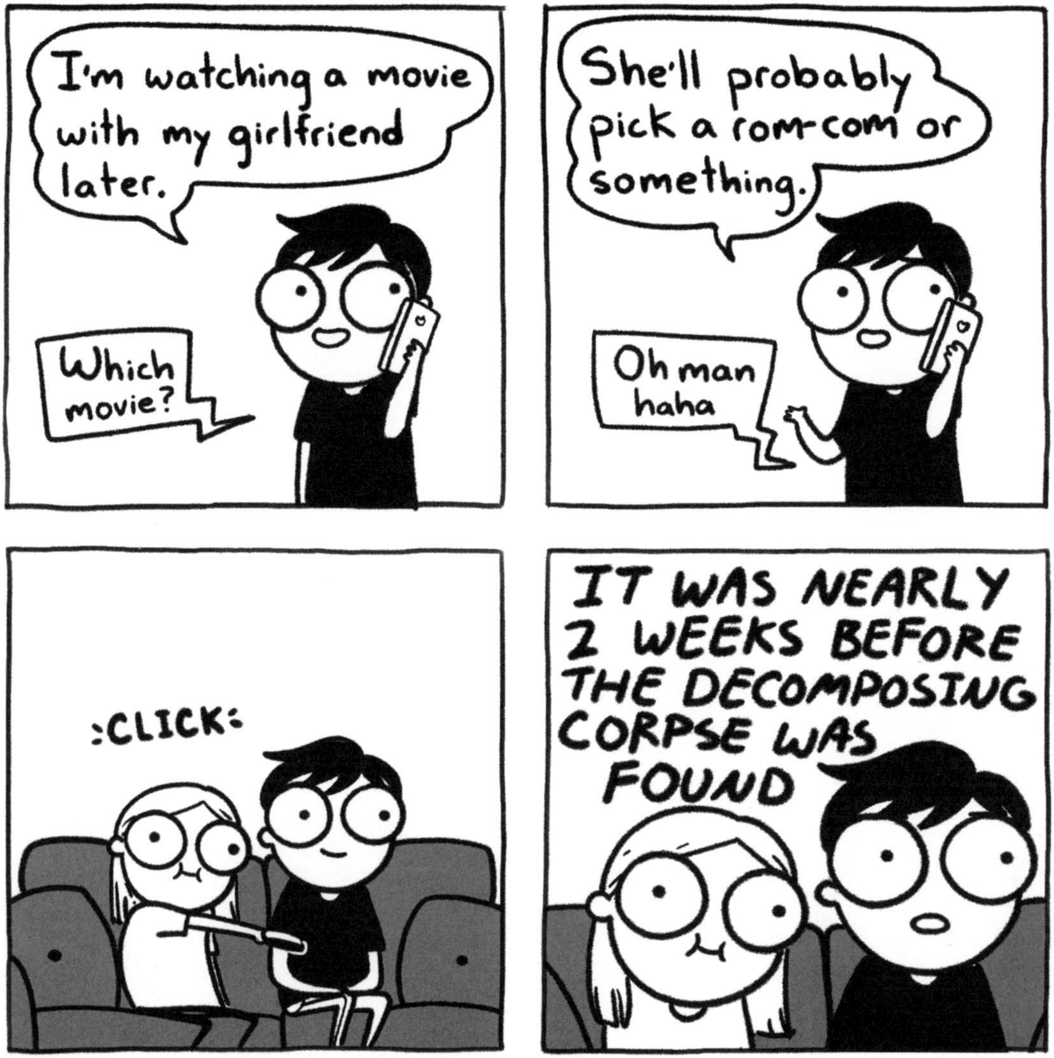
I'm watching a movie with my girlfriend later.
Which movie?
She'll probably pick a rom-com or something.
Oh man haha
:CLICK:
IT WAS NEARLY 2 WEEKS BEFORE THE DECOMPOSING CORPSE WAS FOUND

Raven

Bat

A bit **MORBID**, don't you think? Which one of you is making these?

DIFFERING LOVE LANGUAGES

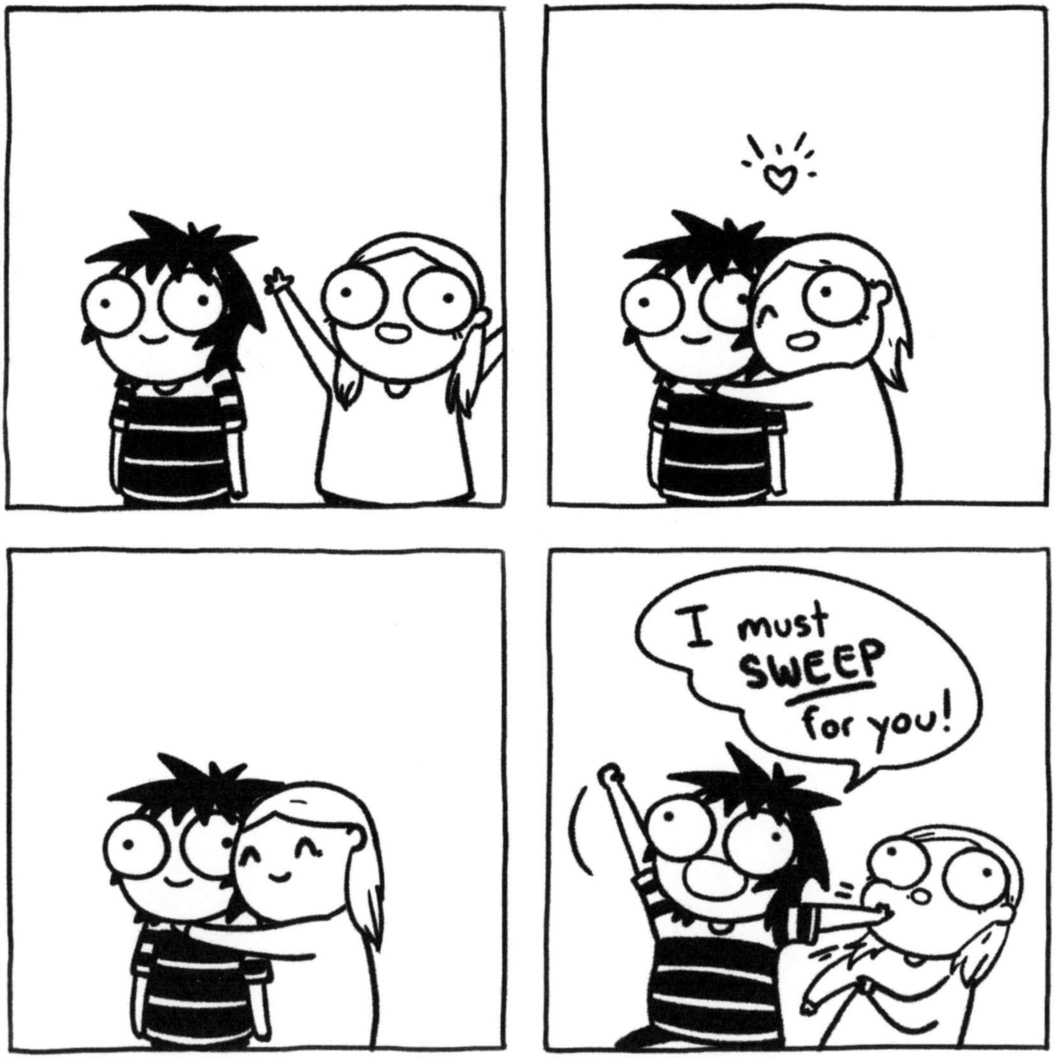
I must SWEEP for you!

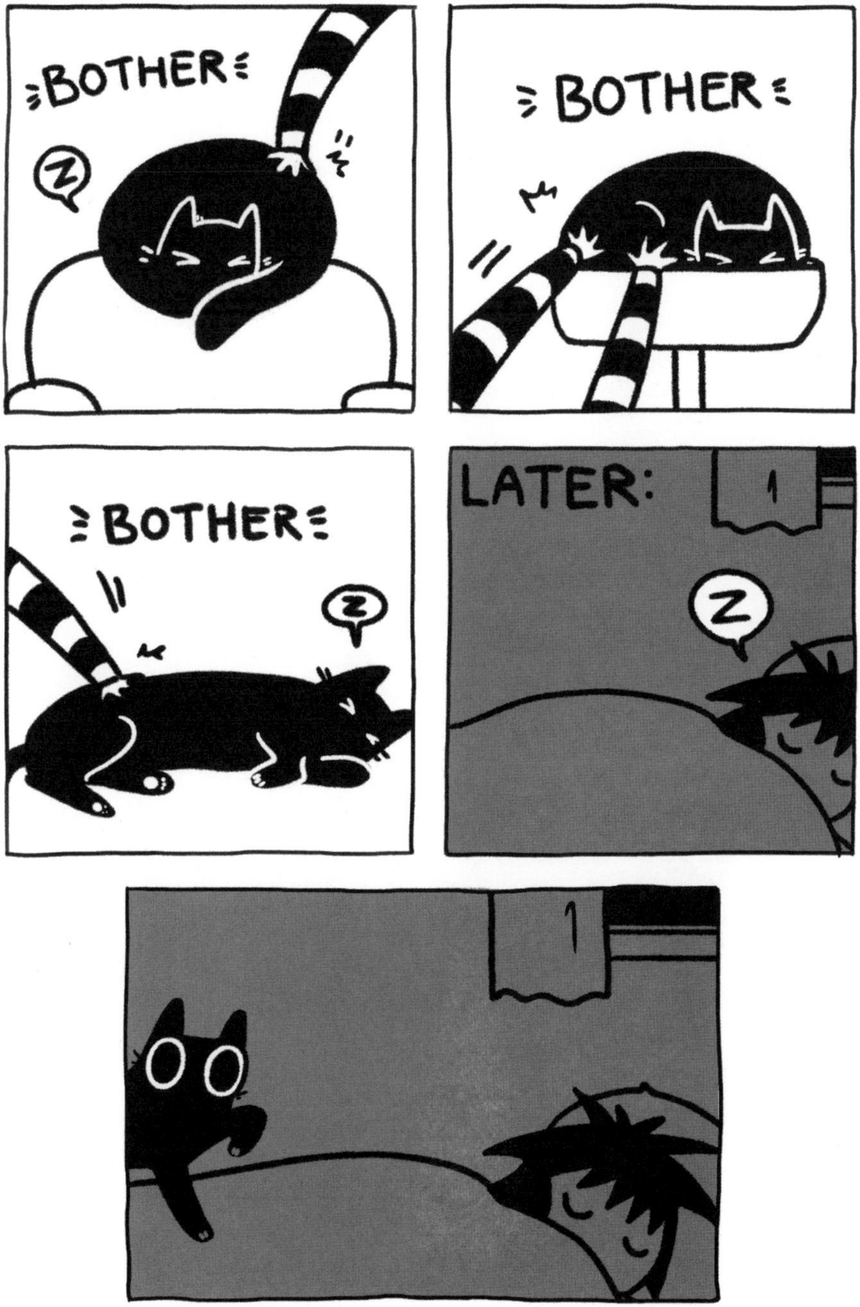
BOTHER
BOTHER
BOTHER
LATER:

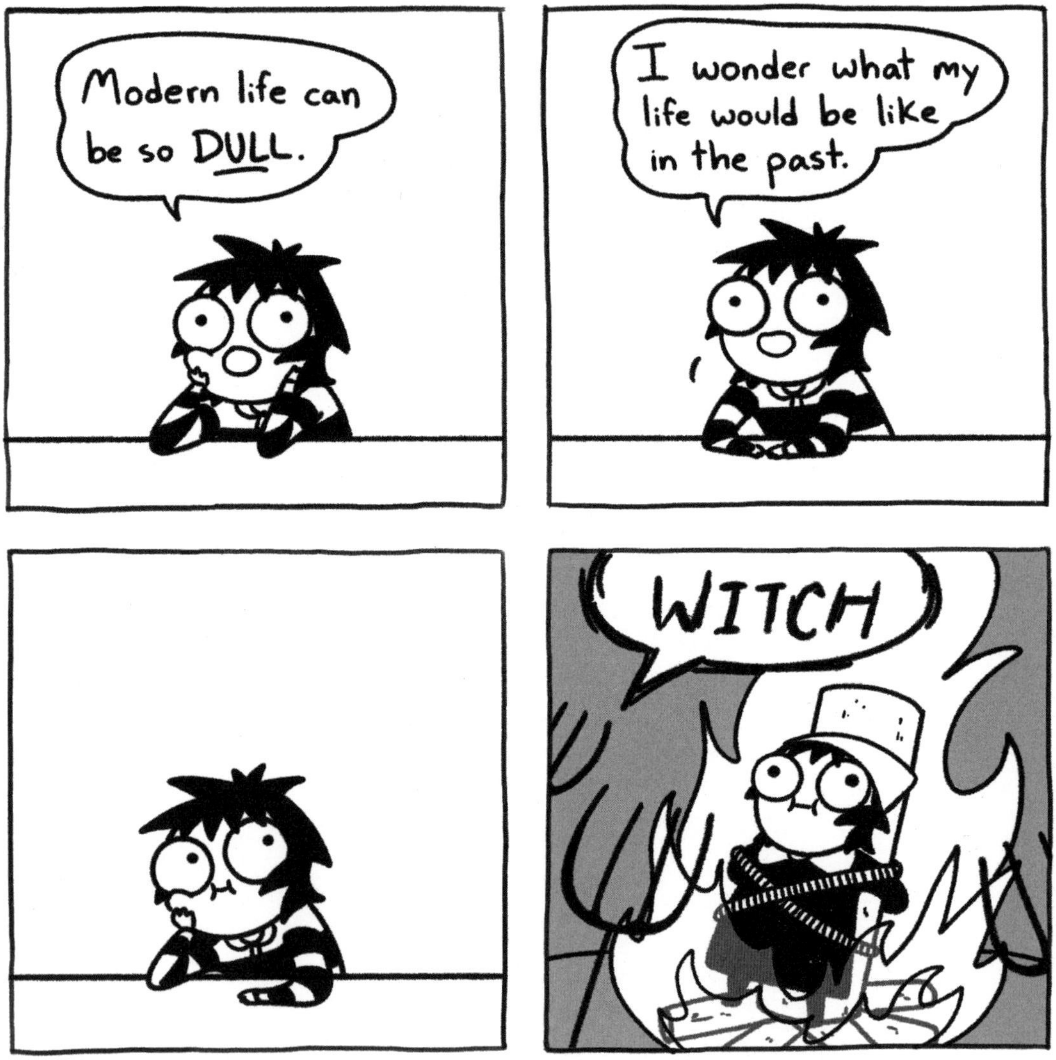
Modern life can be so DULL.
I wonder what my life would be like in the past.
WITCH

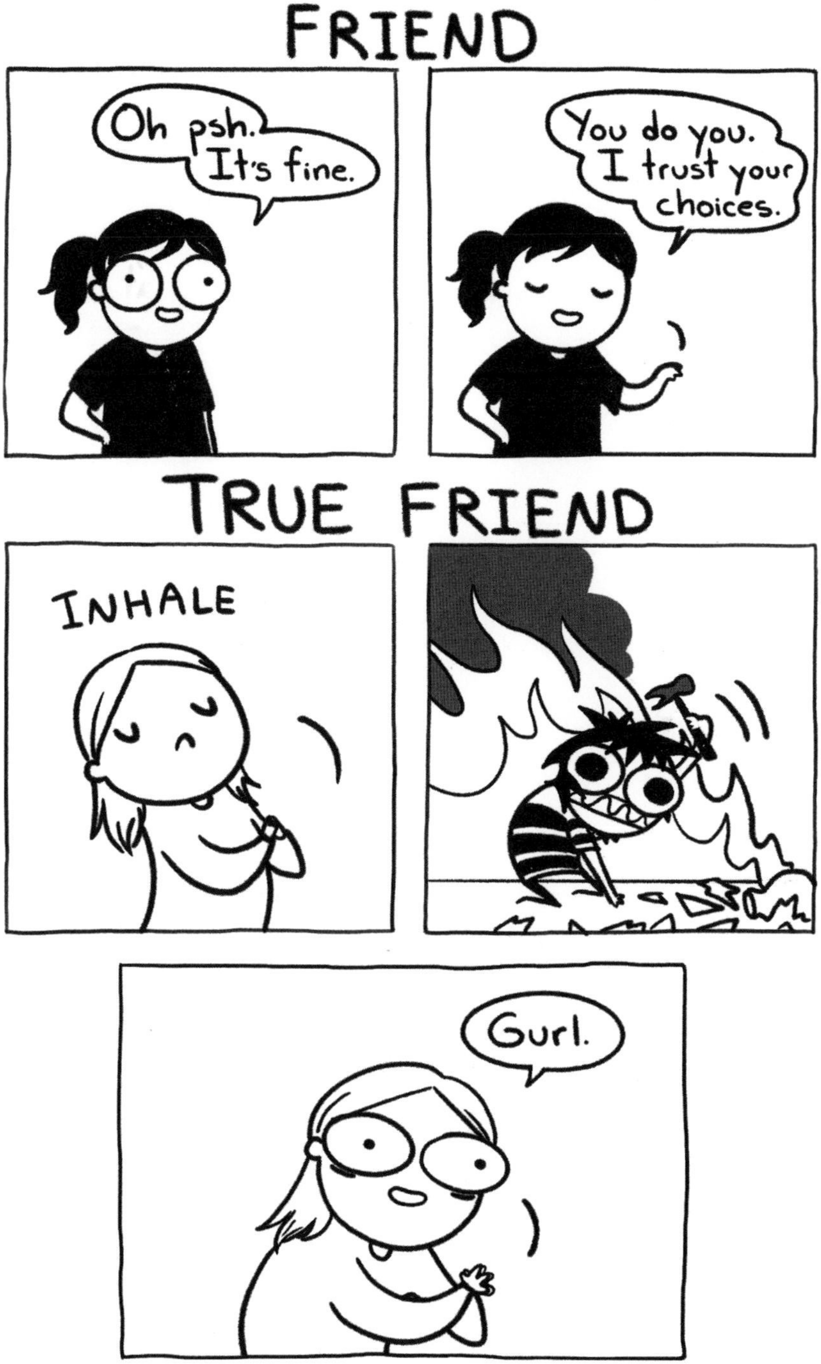
FRIEND
Oh psh. It's fine.
You do you. I trust your choices.
TRUE FRIEND
INHALE
Gurl.

Ma'am it is time for your mental aptitude test.
Can you tell me what this is?
THAT! Is a CHONK.
She's gone.
An absolute UNIT.

BEING MULTILINGUAL:
EXPECTATION
Which language to read Goethe in next hmmm...
REALITY
I am dumb in 3 languages

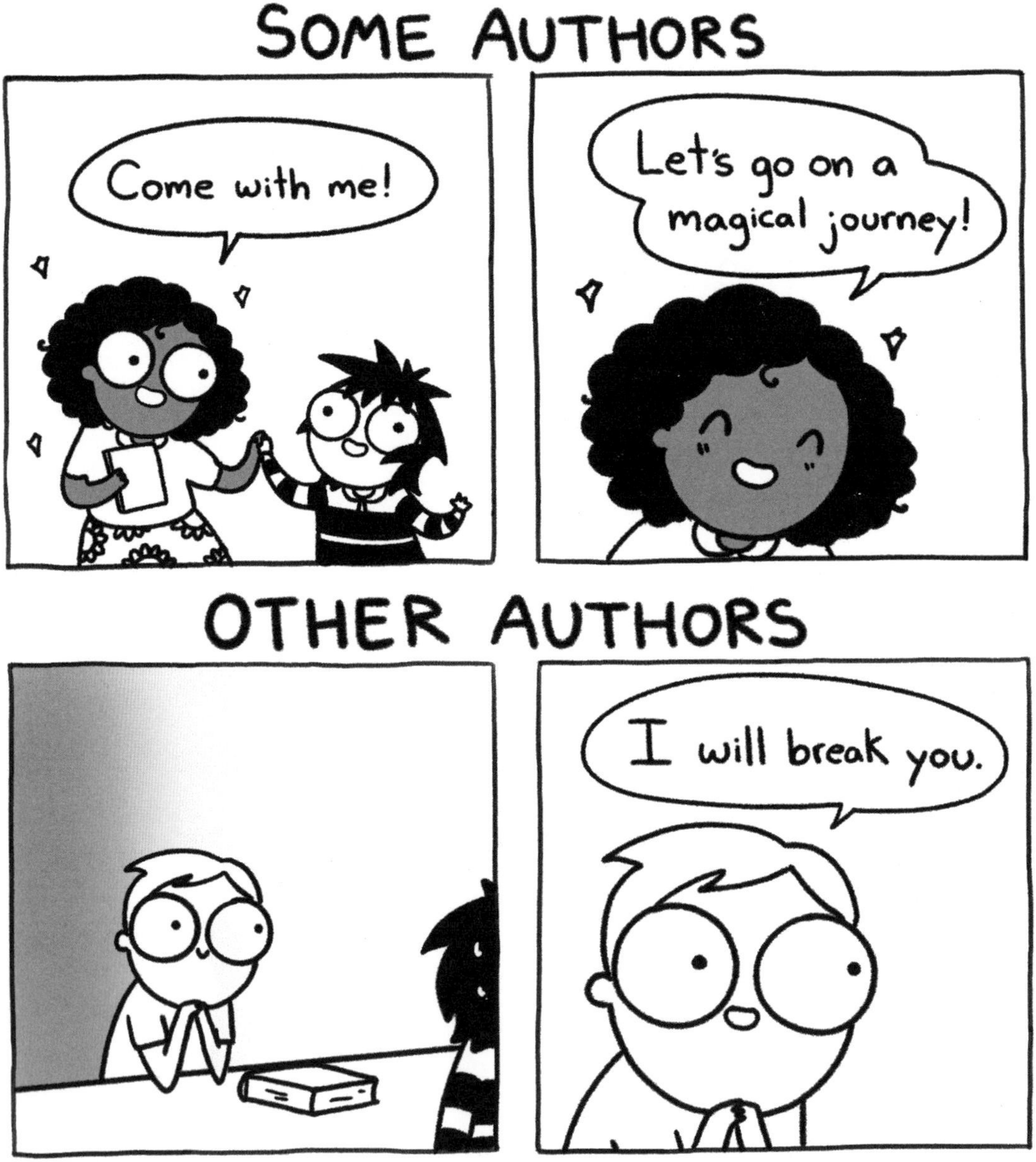
SOME AUTHORS
Come with me!
Let's go on a magical journey!
OTHER AUTHORS
I will break you.

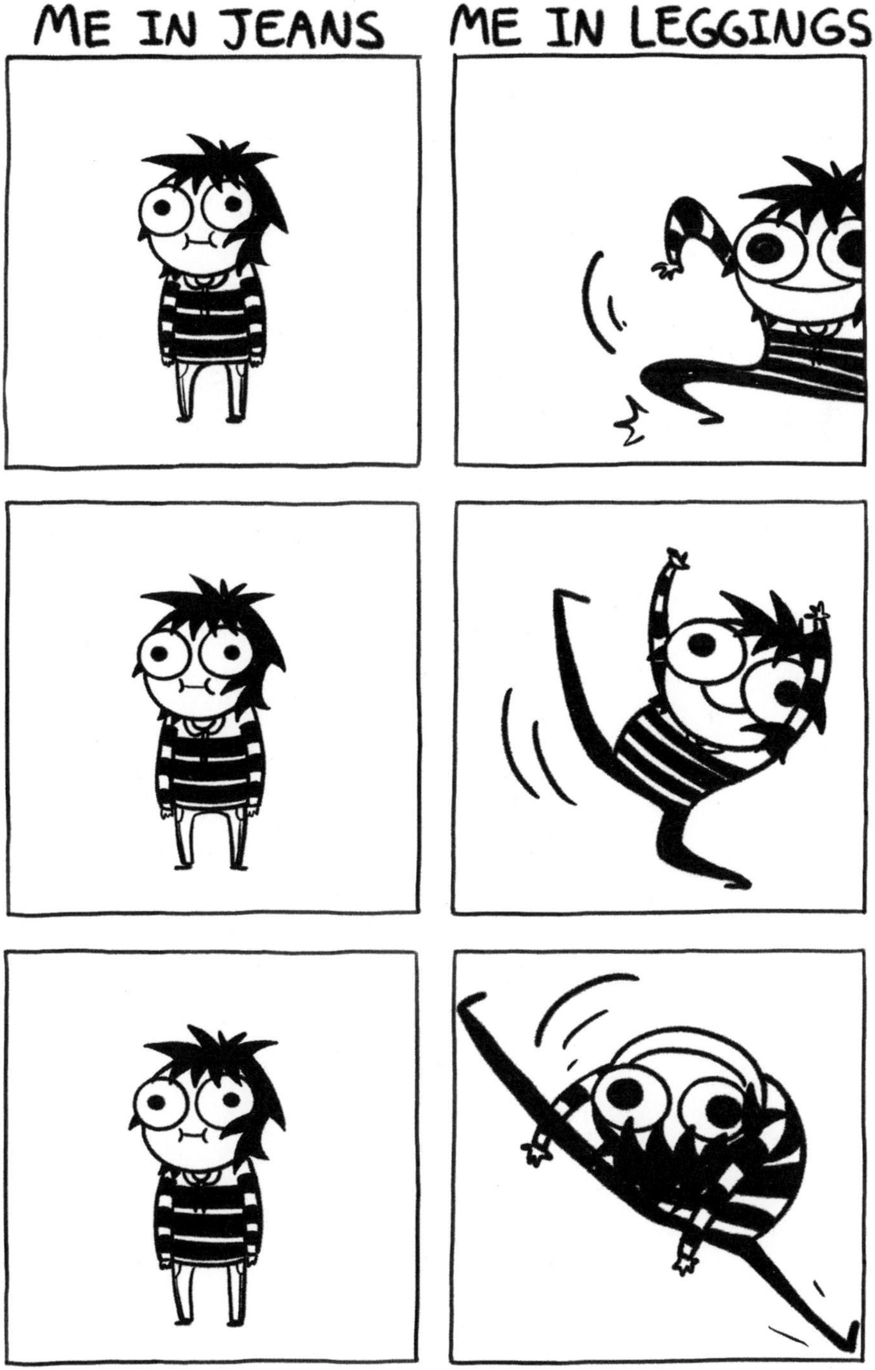
ME IN JEANS
ME IN LEGGINGS

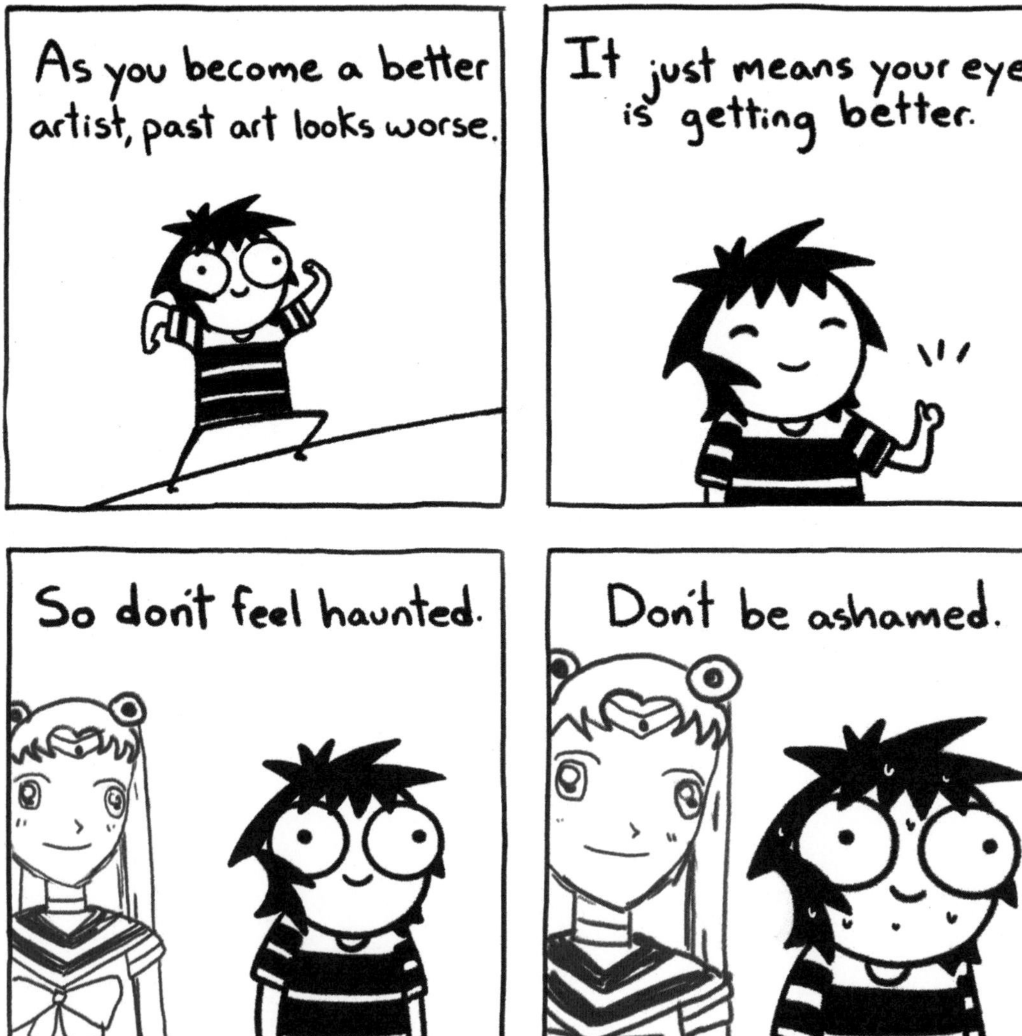
As you become a better artist, past art looks worse.
It just means your eye is getting better.
So don't feel haunted.
Don't be ashamed.

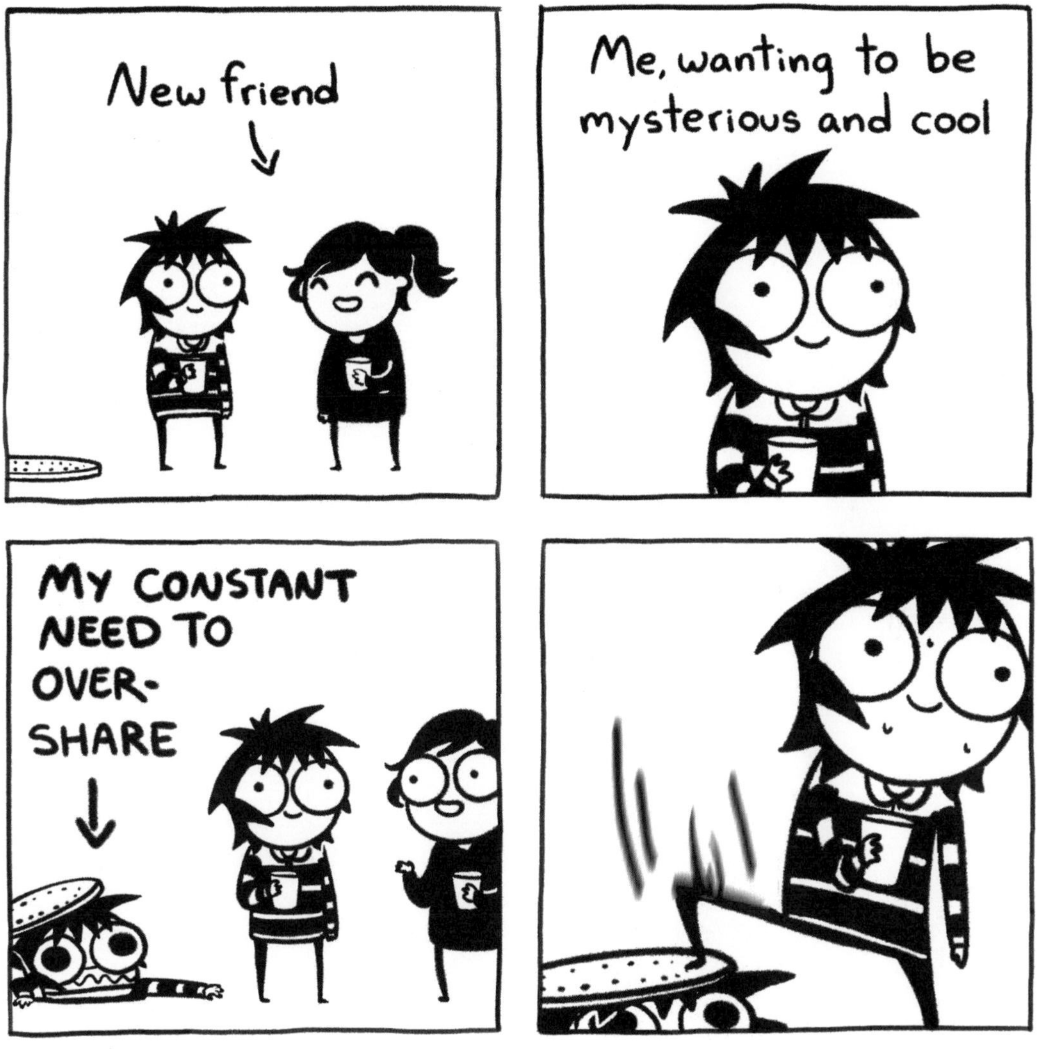
New friend
Me, wanting to be mysterious and cool
MY CONSTANT NEED TO OVER-SHARE

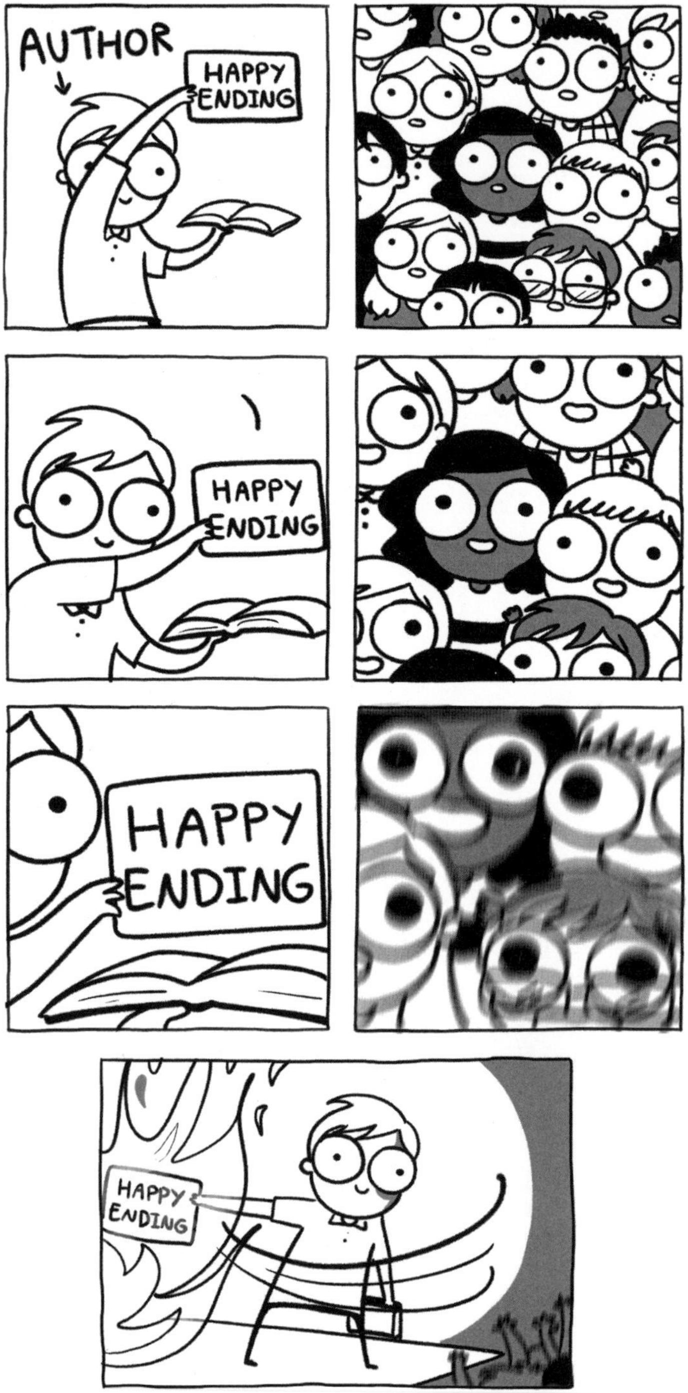
AUTHOR
HAPPY ENDING
HAPPY ENDING
HAPPY ENDING
HAPPY ENDING

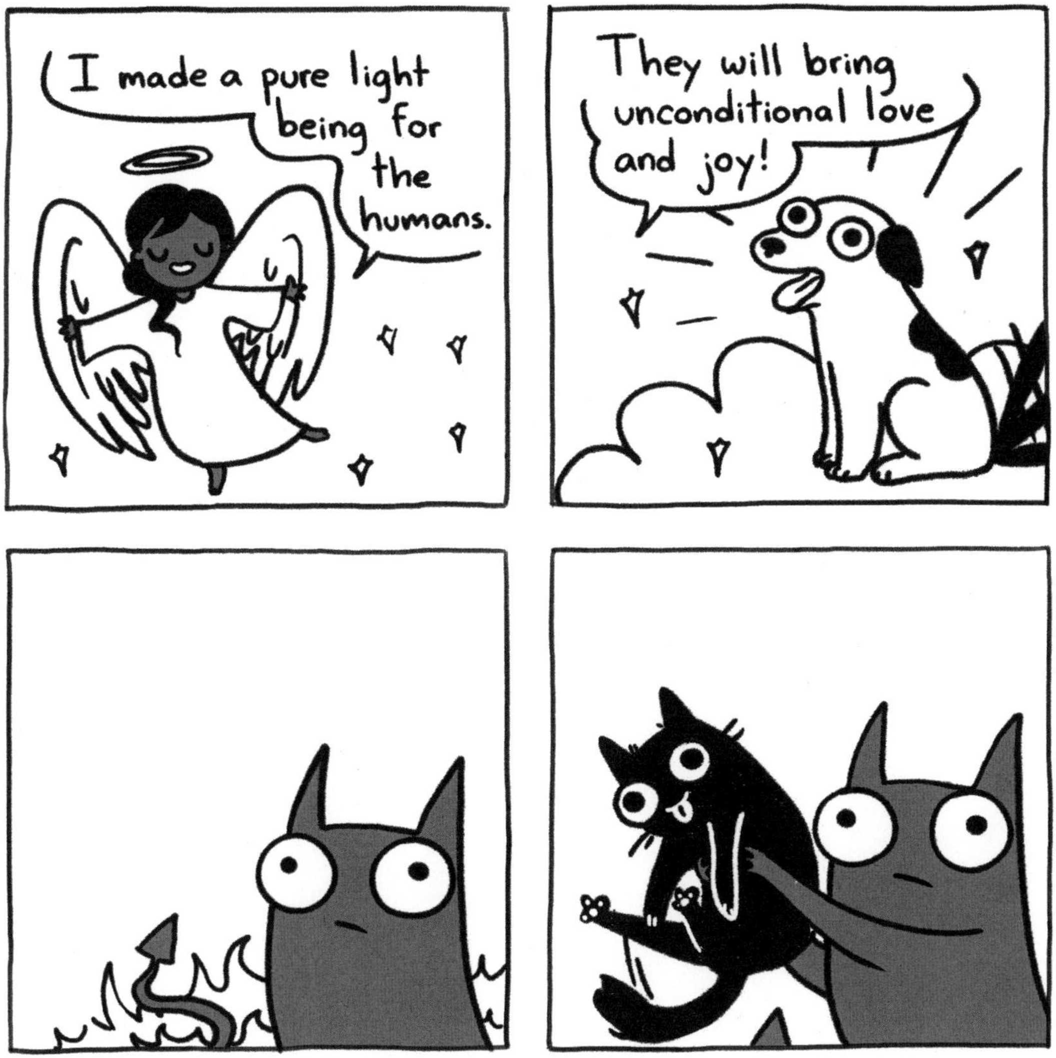
I made a pure light being for the humans.
They will bring unconditional love and joy!

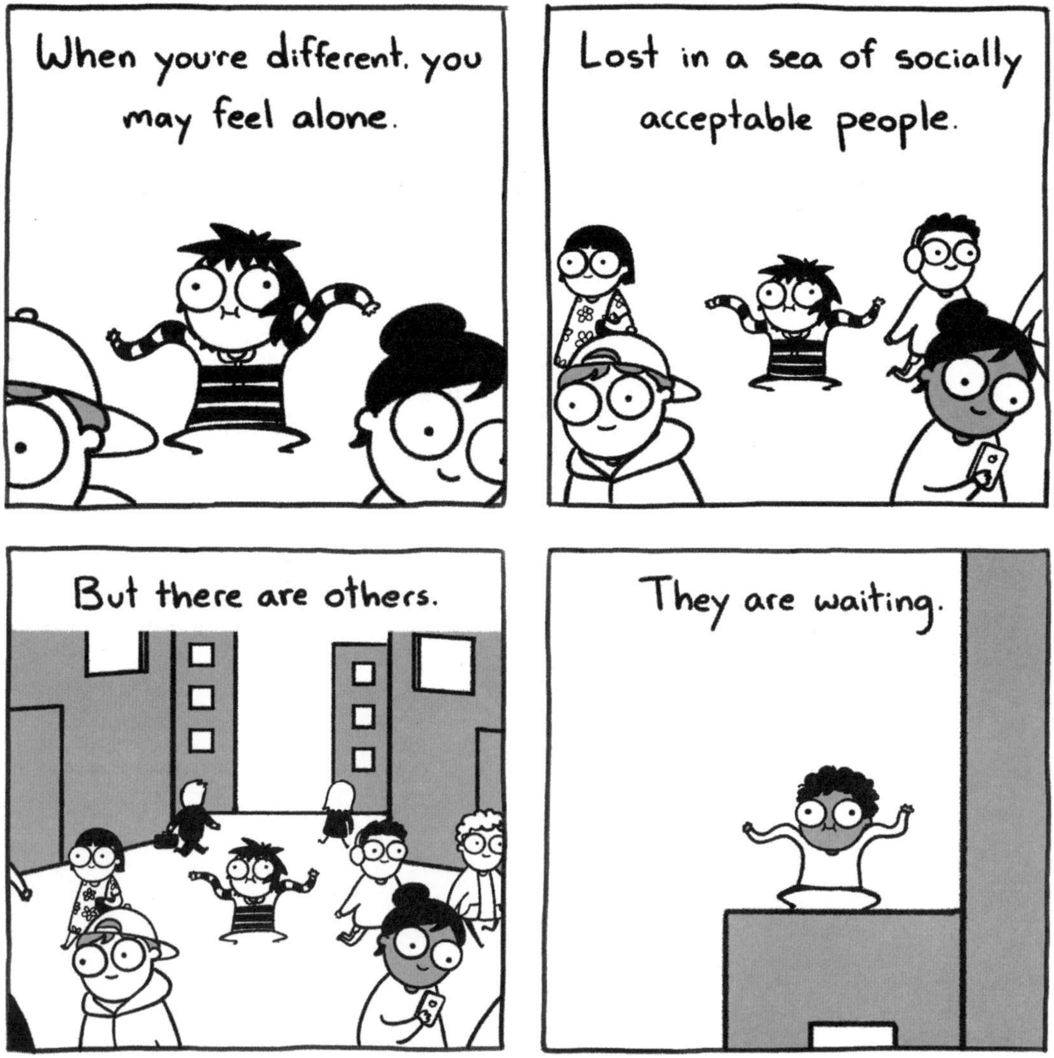
When you're different, you may feel alone.
Lost in a sea of socially acceptable people.
But there are others.
They are waiting.